THINK LIKE A MARKETER

HOW A SHIFT IN MINDSET CAN CHANGE EVERYTHING FOR YOUR BUSINESS

PRAISE FOR
THINK LIKE A MARKETER

"For years, I've been telling my recruiting clients to think like a marketer to improve their ability to attract high-quality candidates. I gave them examples of companies doing it well and some general advice. But, I never had a great resource for them. Until now. *Think Like a Marketer* is a game changer. When I received a short sample copy (Kate's thoughtful way of practicing what she preaches in the chapter on 'sampling strategies'), I expected a typical marketing primer. I was so wrong! I devoured that sample and wanted MORE!!! Like right now, this minute, temper-tantrum kind of more. I got my greedy little fingers on an advance copy and devoured that. Each chapter has incredible insights and takeaways. You'll love the 'Ask Yourself' sections at the end of each chapter, which masterfully train non-marketing brains to *think like a marketer*. Kate is a genius!"

Rebecca Barnes-Hogg, SPHR, SHRM-SCP
Founder of YOLO Insights® and Author of *The YOLO Principle: The Ultimate Hiring Guide for Small Business*

"What I most enjoyed about Kate Colbert's book, *Think Like a Marketer*, is that it marries her personal voice along with concrete examples of the points she so powerfully makes. The writing style of this book is a reflection of Kate herself: intelligent, thoughtful, and articulate. She offers great insights for those who are not marketers and good reminders for those of us who have been doing this important work for a long time."

Karen Abruzzi
Director of Marketing, EBSCO Industries

"Kate Colbert has been a remarkable help to me over the many years she has served as my marketing advisor. Reading her book left me with the sense we were having one of our regular conversations, where I learn so much from her. For sole proprietors like me, the advice she provides truly makes the difference between real success versus just muddling along. I consider it very generous of her to have taken the time to share her knowledge and experience with a broader audience through *Think Like a Marketer*, which is an exceptionally strong book. I will make good use of this resource, likely with many notes and stickies throughout."

David Kushner
Advisor to CEOs & Governing Boards;
Merger, Alliance & Restructuring Expert

"An MBA in a book? That's exactly what I consider this to be! Kate takes her successful business experience and shows us how developing a 'marketing mindset' was key to her success, and will do the same for you. I've been in sales and marketing my entire career. Trust me — this book can help you to grow your business!"

Lois Creamer
Marketing Expert for Speakers and
Author of *Book More Business: Make Money Speaking*

"What I love about *Think Like a Marketer* is that it gives business owners both ideas *and* guardrails. As an entrepreneur, I sometimes struggle with where to draw the line when I get excited about a new idea. Colbert's book has helped stretch my thinking, and has gently reminded me that sometimes I need to call on a trained professional."

Amy C. Waninger

Founder and CEO of Lead at Any Level, LLC, and Author of *Network Beyond Bias: Making Diversity a Competitive Advantage for Your Career*

"After three decades of climbing the corporate ladder, I finally decided to officially start my own consulting firm. When friends and colleagues ask what has been my biggest challenge, I always respond with one word: marketing! I suck at it — but now I have hope! Kate Colbert to the rescue. *Think Like a Marketer* will take my business to the next level. I can't wait to channel Kate's experience, ideas and principles to attract and keep more customers. Buying this book will be the best investment I can make in the future of my business!"

Kathy Koultourides

Certified Professional in Learning and Performance, Founder of KKNOW HOW LLC, and Author of *Lucifer Leaders: The Hidden Cost of Deviant Behavior in the Sales Force*

"Having worked directly with Kate and having received her expert marketing consultation, I knew *Think Like a Marketer* would be loaded with valuable information and insights. Despite expecting greatness, I am still surprised at how clearly Kate's friendly, engaging and knowledgeable voice comes through in her writing, and what a pleasant experience her voice creates despite covering a topic that to me has never felt 'fun' to study."

Jason Sackett, PCC, LCSW, CEAP

Executive Coach, Trainer, and Author of *Compassion@Work: Creating Workplaces that Engage the Human Spirit*

"Kate Colbert imprinted her expertise in the marketing world long before the publication of *Think Like a Marketer*. Her book is the culmination of decades of experience, of steeping herself in research for the benefit of her clients and herself, of delving deep into the psyche and motivation of the consumer to deliver the most seductive strategy and content possible. In *Think Like a Marketer*, she has, in her impeccable style, laid out digestible sections, highlighting the key components that every marketer or business person needs to know and practice to reach their professional aims and to ensure their clients never leave. Read this to slam dunk your marketing missive."

Hilary Jastram
CEO, Founder, J. Hill Marketing & Creative Services

"Whether you are a seasoned marketer or a small business person just starting out, *Think Like a Marketer* has something for you. The real-world examples of companies, brands, and business leaders make the material come alive and deliver an extra measure of credibility to the advice. I love the way you can skip around the pages, depending on what's needed at the moment. As a seasoned marketer, I appreciated the new perspectives and insights; for the person new to the business world, this book offers a roadmap for transforming your thinking, your processes, and your results."

Joyce Gioia
Celebrity Futurist, Professional Speaker, and Author of *Experience Rules: How Positive Experiences Will Drive Profit into the Future*

"*Think Like a Marketer* is a marketing degree in a book. No matter your industry or position, you must be a marketer in today's world, and Kate Colbert's book gives you all the skills you need. From storytelling to sampling to networking to getting the most out of conference attendance and everything in between, Kate covers it and explains — in simple terms — why and how to step up your marketing game. *Think Like a Marketer* is written conversationally, so you'll feel like Kate is speaking directly to you. I keep reference books like the *AP Stylebook* within easy reach on my desk; *Think Like a Marketer* joins that collection of "can't live without" business/ reference books I use daily. Read this book with pen and paper handy, because Kate's tips will spark many ideas for marketing your business that you won't want to lose. *Think Like a Marketer* is truly a 'learn it today, use it today' kind of book."

Jessica Gardner

Fundraising and Event Professional, Community Builder, and *ChicagoNow* "Little Merry Sunshine" Blogger

"'Relationships begin with hello ... and how you say it matters.' This is sage advice from Kate Colbert — advice that she embraces and demonstrates in her new book, *Think Like a Marketer*, as well as in person, when working with clients and colleagues. What most impressed me about this book is Kate's willingness to be vulnerable and bold enough to let her true personality, passion and enthusiasm shine through while packing in a wealth of marketing knowledge and actionable steps that marketers and non-marketers alike can start employing *right now* to shift their businesses — and even their own careers — from mediocre to meaningfully different."

Barb Cahoon Wang, JD, Northwestern University

Founder and Consultant, Inflection Point Communications

"A business lacks possibility for reaching its fullest potential when its leader lacks the right mindset. And it's never too late to 'change your mind.' Kate Colbert's book, *Think Like a Marketer,* demonstrates how mindset shifts can be life-changing for leaders and game-changing for your business. As a marketing professional myself, I couldn't agree more! So much is packed into these pages that an investment in this book will set any business up for more success than they dream possible. Every business leader and entrepreneur looking to set themselves — and their organizations — apart should harness the knowledge Kate pours into each chapter of this impactful and transformative book!"

Stephanie Feger
Communications and Marketing Consultant, Professional Speaker, and Author of *Color Today Pretty: An Inspirational Guide to Living a Life in Perspective*

"If you are a busy entrepreneur like I am, you know you need to keep focused on marketing. But how do you do it when you wear so many hats? The answer is simple: read Kate Colbert's book, *Think Like a Marketer*! I love Kate's practical, actionable advice for busy entrepreneurs in this easy-to-read book. If you want to grow your business, *Think Like a Marketer*!"

Cathy Fyock
The Business Book Strategist and Author of *Blog2Book: Repurposing Content to Discover the Book You've Already Written*

"Kate Colbert takes a discussion of 'everyday' marketing principles and elevates it to a new level, making her insights accessible to business professionals across industries and at different junctures in their careers. A MUST read for marketing novices and seasoned veterans alike."

Dawn Smith

Independent Wellness Coach

"Kate gets it. She realizes we are all marketers of something and that we need help to think differently. I enjoy how she shares her expertise and invites us to connect it to our own industry and brand. Her knowledge and practical approach gives the reader space to think about their company or role, from the perspective of the ultimate consumer — the customer or client. What are you doing to be meaningfully different from what your competitors are offering? If you care about adding long-term value to your customer, you have to dig-in and *Think Like a Marketer*."

Ann Brown

Business Author and Founder of The Development Edge

"Easy to read with great content. A game changer for anyone running or starting a business!"

Tonia Morris

Speaker, Multigenerational Trainer, Coach, and Author of *Compassion@Work: Creating Workplaces That Engage the Human Spirit* and *Before You Say "I Do" to Entrepreneurship: What You Need to Know Before You Leave Your 9-to-5 Job*

"Kate is easily one of the wisest marketing and business development experts I know, and *Think Like a Marketer* provides an opportunity to learn from the best.

Many people cringe at the word 'marketing,' but we often forget that marketing is simply, at its core, about understanding *people*. Kate has the extraordinary ability to take some of the mystery out of what makes people tick, what keeps them engaged and what drives their buying decisions. Regardless of your industry or specialty, *Think Like a Marketer* provides myriad actionable ways for you to connect (or reconnect!) more effectively with your customers, and, ultimately, be more successful at what *you* do best.

Kate's easy-going, conversational writing style captivates, and before you know it, you are planning all the ways in which you can incorporate her guidance into your business plans. Believe it or not, you might even start thinking that marketing is fun ... *like a marketer!*"

Courtney Hudson
Marketing, Branding and Design Consultant; Professional Services Marketing Specialist; and Founder of Lorenne Marketing & Design

THINK LIKE A
MARKETER

HOW A SHIFT IN MINDSET
CAN CHANGE EVERYTHING
FOR YOUR BUSINESS

KATE COLBERT

SILVER TREE
PUBLISHING

THINK LIKE A MARKETER
5 PRINCIPLES TO GUIDE YOU

SHIFT YOUR MINDSET AND
CHANGE EVERYTHING FOR YOUR BUSINESS

Embrace the actions and attitudes that can take you and your organization from status quo to success story, from busy to profitable, and from mediocre to meaningfully different. This book teaches you to *think like a marketer*.

Thinking like a marketer requires that you:

1. Communicate for connection and meaning, not just to transact sales

2. Live and die by your customer insights

3. Market in a way that's strategy-religious and tactic-agnostic

4. Create cultures and processes that align with your brand

5. Do everything in service of maintaining a virtuous cycle of *creating value* for the customer while *capturing value* for you.

DEDICATION

To the men and women whose marketing minds informed my own. Your innovative ways of caring for customers, telling meaningful brand stories and capturing sustainable value for your organizations taught me that marketing is far more than shameless promotion. Your wild successes (and even your failures) have helped me understand the risks and rewards of this vital work. And your passion and dedication for connecting the marketplace with products and services customers need and crave is admirable beyond words. You have taught me so that I can teach others. *I thank you.*

And for my mom, who was perhaps the first person — and surely the most important one — to teach me to think like a marketer, I gratefully dedicate this book. When I was rewriting billboards in the backseat of a Datsun, analyzing television commercials while sitting cross-legged on the shag carpeting with my brother, and questioning pricing strategies in the grocery store aisles as a child, she encouraged me and saw what I didn't see until decades later … that I was born to be a marketer. Thank you, Mom, for always believing in me and supporting my career. I love you. *I hope I have done you proud.*

TABLE OF CONTENTS

03 Give It Away!   65

**(Because They Can't Know if They Love You if They've
Never Sampled Your Product)**

04 Don't Give it ALL Away, for Heaven's Sake!   75

(Monetize It!)

05 Love (and Protect!) Your Database or Lose Your Company   85

A LETTER TO MY READER

Perhaps we've met before. Maybe you're a client or a former colleague, a classmate from a shared alma mater or a friend of a friend. Maybe you've been in the audience during a presentation or workshop I led, have followed my blog or met me at a professional conference. If that's the case, thank you for your continued connection, confidence or support. But if you're like most readers of *Think Like a Marketer*, your decision to read this book is what brought us to "hello." And it's truly my pleasure and honor to meet you. Let me give you a little backstory about me, the work I do and the life I live — I think it will give you meaningful context for what you're about to read.

I'M AN ACCIDENTAL MARKETER

I cringed a little when I wrote that subheading. Because the idea of being an "accidental" anything, to me, seems as if I mean I am the beneficiary of "dumb luck" or that I don't have the smarts, experience or character to be where I am, to do what I do or to succeed as I have.

But, you see, I *am* an accidental marketer. Sort of. I started my career with the intention to write and to teach others to write ... period. I finished my Master of Arts degree in English composition and comparative literature with a starry-eyed plan to become a college English professor ... forever and ever, amen. After just a few years of classroom experience in outstanding institutions, I was ready to do more. So, I stopped grading freshman essays and started writing articles and editing columns for a high-tech industry magazine.

It was work I loved, and it challenged me immensely. There I was, breaking stories about the invention of Bluetooth technology and touring silicon wafer fabrication facilities to uncover the next big thing in mobile phone evolution and automotive electronics. And without realizing it, I was also surrounded by the worlds of sales and marketing, working on the other side of the desk, as it were, from other vital communications professionals — the marketing and public relations representatives of top companies in the United States and around the globe. Without ever having written a press release myself, I quickly became an expert in press releases. And without ever having planned an event, designed a trade show booth, executed a marketing campaign, directed a radio commercial or photo shoot, or developed a marketing strategy, I became a discriminating consumer of all things marketing. It was my job to absorb the marketing that companies were enthusiastically targeting to magazine editors like me (so that I could generate third-party media content validating those messages, visuals and brand promises). I was surrounded by communications professionals but didn't see myself as one.

**I was surrounded by communications professionals ...
but didn't see myself as one.**

When the dot-com bubble burst and the world of tech suffered great losses, my time writing about semiconductor packaging came to an abrupt end. The companies that had once been flush with cash for trade publication advertising struggled and recalibrated their strategies. The marketing budgets dried up, and so did my job.

Suddenly unemployed, I needed to stay busy and generate an income, so I started freelancing — first as a writer and an editor, and then more broadly as a communications consultant. Quite accidentally, I founded what was to become my life's work — a communications consultancy called Silver Tree Communications, LLC. I stopped being a consumer of PR and marketing and began generating it, representing some of the same technology companies that had previously pitched me for stories. I also began developing marketing and PR strategies for clients in industries as diverse as healthcare, professional sports and higher education. I performed this exciting work full time for about a year, then as a "side gig" when I landed a new job that could provide a stable, predictable paycheck and fringe benefits. But I knew I'd come back to Silver Tree when I could. Silver Tree was my anchor and my love from the very start. Now, 16 years after its founding, it's what makes everything — even this book — possible for me. (And it turned out that my mom's hunch when I was a child — that I had an inherent love and knack for marketing — was right, after all.)

It wasn't until about six years later — mid-way between the founding of my company and when I would come back to it for good — that I first heard that dreaded phrase: *accidental marketer.* I was just getting settled into a new role as director of marketing at a private graduate business school when the chief marketing officer told me that my career path struck him as an unusual one. He believed I had arrived there quite by "accident," that because I hadn't enrolled in business school full time in my early 20s (but, rather, had spent several years honing my craft as a writer, marketer and professional communicator before applying that practical expertise to the classroom explorations in business school), I lacked the "pedigree" he sought in the people he hired. *Pedigree?* *Like a dog?* Listen ... I love dogs more than the average person (#truth), but I'd never been compared to one before. I was livid. Offended. Wondered why he'd bothered to hire me. But dog comparisons aside, he was right. I became a great marketer by layering valuable experiences upon one another ... I went from great writer to great communications expert, to great marketer and public relations pro. And I did it all without any of my four college degrees having included a major or minor in marketing.

This book will offer you insight into those things that can take you from here to there, from busy to profitable, and from mediocre to meaningfully different.

So, why am I telling you this story? Because many readers of this book have something in common with me — you never intended (or intend) to become marketers. You just want to be great at your jobs. I suspect most of you already are. Like every vital business function, we all need to know at least a little something about marketing if we're going to be successful for the long haul. This book will offer you insight into those things that can take you from here to there, from busy to profitable, and from mediocre to meaningfully different. While you have surely sometimes needed a great marketing agency, a great marketing consultant and/or a great marketing employee, what you need first, most and always is *a great marketing mindset.* I assure you that it can and will change everything about your business. It doesn't matter whether you're a management consultant or the owner of a diner that serves the best biscuits and gravy in town, the ability to think like a marketer will give you a competitive edge, and you don't need a degree in marketing to get there. (Hell, I own a marketing company and don't have a degree in marketing either!)

THINKING "LIKE A ... " MAKES US ALL STRONGER

No matter how good we are at what we do, there are risks inherent in not understanding the full business ecosystem and in not fully appreciating how to talk with and work with people in other functional areas.

If you run the IT department, it helps to know a little bit about accounting and whether a server is considered capital equipment, or desktop computers are depreciated over time or expensed in the current fiscal year.

If you're an oncologist, it helps to spend some time with the operations leaders at your hospital to understand the practicalities of scheduling treatments that require inpatient recovery time. It also helps to understand the responsibilities of the legal and risk management teams as it relates to the clinical trial you'd like to lead.

If you're an accountant, it helps to understand the people, projects and strategies behind the numbers. Knowing how a proposed investment is projected by the customer care division to reduce the cost of ongoing client services by 30% is vital to working within the greater context of your organization.

Together, we succeed. But it's difficult to succeed in business — whether you're a business owner or a manager, director or executive — because we were educated *separately* (by "majors!") and we work largely in silos. We have spent our careers gaining more experience and professional development (conferences, certifications, etc.) in our own areas of practice. We go deeper into our areas of functional expertise without ever purposefully broadening ourselves.

This limited business viewpoint is what drove me to earn
a professional MBA degree when I was in my mid-30s. I didn't want
an MBA *credential*; I needed the *perspective* that the MBA curriculum
would offer. I needed to "think like a ... " (insert business function here: finance professional, lawyer, operations manager, CEO,
IT expert, and more). You see, when I first realized that a narrow
viewpoint was essentially career quicksand, I was the director of
communications at a Chicago-area medical sciences university. No
one in the institution would have argued that I knew an enticing
brochure when I saw one or that I could write a compelling script for
a radio commercial. They thought I was a good "marketer." But they
didn't see me as a *leader* because I didn't speak their language.

I didn't have a seat at the executive table because I hadn't earned it
by learning to place my work — my priorities, my requests, my needs
— in the contexts of every other department around me. It's not that
they wanted me to make a permanent career move — to go from
marketing to IT, for example. They wanted me to walk the walk and
talk the talk everywhere I went — to be a marketer who understood
how her work fit into the rest of the organization. They wanted me to
have the kind of elevated, 30,000-foot viewpoint of how all the pieces
of the operation fit together — the kind of viewpoint that drives innovative, relevant thinking.[1]

Getting my MBA at Lake Forest Graduate School of Management
(an institution with business-leader faculty and a practical curriculum) allowed me to fill those vital gaps. Despite the fact that I might
never work in the manufacturing sector, I learned about addressing

---

[1] Be sure to check out Rich Horwath's compelling book *Elevate: The Three
    Disciplines of Advanced Strategic Thinking* for a deep exploration of the type
    of strategic thinking and broad viewpoint that makes for great leadership of
    successful companies.

bottlenecks caused by people and production equipment running in a suboptimal way. I learned about finance and economics, strategy, negotiation and accounting. As I learned to think like my classmates, I could connect with them more meaningfully. And as they learned to think like me, my ideas and work had new relevance.

No one in the institution would have argued that I knew an enticing brochure when I saw one or that I could write a compelling script for a radio commercial. They thought I was a good "marketer." But they didn't see me as a *leader* because I didn't speak their language.

If you, too, have the chance to broaden your viewpoint, do it. Shadow someone in a different department or function at work. Take a class outside your profession or college major. Seek mentorship or professional development in an area outside your own expertise.

I decided to write *Think Like a Marketer* because my clients often tell me that the shifts in mindset that they have adopted after working with me have changed everything for their businesses. And I wanted to make that shift possible for more people and more companies.

Thinking like a marketer is, in my opinion, critical for business leaders and owners. I have no doubt that learning to think like *other* professions will provide similar breakthroughs. For that reason, I hope that experts in other areas will consider how a "think like a ..." book in *their* area of expertise could similarly help business owners and leaders. I hope you'll write those books because I'd love to read them. (Perhaps my company will even publish them! Feel free to contact me at Editor@PublishWithSilverTree.com if you have an idea for a book in a *Think Like a ...* series. I'd enjoy hearing from you.)

YOU HAVE QUESTIONS ... THE MINDSET PROVIDES ANSWERS

There's just simply too much at stake, at your company and in your career, for you not to "think like a marketer." Having a narrow mindset — one that fails to incorporate the considerations that a great marketer would never overlook — can cause you to make costly mistakes in communicating with customers, crafting and promoting your products, how you tell your story, and in how you spend your advertising or promotional dollars.

Thinking like a marketer will also help you say "no" to low-value projects, activities and expenses, and say "yes" to initiatives that serve your long-term business and career strategies. If you're anything like me, you've got too much on your plate, too many good ideas and too many opportunities knocking (if I might recklessly mix metaphors in this sentence). Taking a litmus test (the question "what would I do if I was *truly* thinking like a marketer in this moment?") has been key to helping me know when to say "no" and when to say "yes." Applying the "think like a marketer" filter to your decisions will help you create value and capture value, every day, for as long as you choose to do the amazing work that drives you. Then, you can take all that value you've captured and go launch something new, craft an encore career after an official "retirement" or buy a yacht. It's up to you!

Can "thinking like a marketer" truly be revolutionary for careers and companies? It depends how you apply these principles and how rigorously you adopt the mindset, but YES. Let the mindset change you, and the mindset will change your business.

Let the mindset change you, and the mindset will change your business.

What else will *thinking like a marketer* do for you? Let me demon-strate what good marketing looks like by telling you, up front, before you've invested even a single hour of reading, what you're "buying" by reading this book — let me attempt to answer the questions that might be on your mind. Ready?

- Can I read this book in a "choose your own adventure" way, jumping ahead to chapters with topics that appeal to me instead of reading it from cover-to-cover?

  YES!   This book was written in a way that invites you to jump from here to there, to scribble in the margins (something my husband considers a sacrilege and I consider "inter-acting with the text!"), dog-ear the pages and stick Post-Its and tape flags all over. It's also full of bite-sized insights that tie the stories and recommendations back to the 5 *Think Like a Marketer* Principles, brainstorming exer-cises called "Ask Yourself," and predictions for the future, which can help keep you ahead of the curve in your business. Go ahead ... dig in, skip around, choose your own reading path.

- Can I apply much of the advice in this book on my own, without a consultant or a marketing agency?

  YES!   Big businesses are often built on small budgets. Let's see how far your investment in this book can take you.

- Do the principles in this book apply to me if I am a one-person consultancy?

  YES!   Some of the clients who I've seen make the most remark-able "think-like-a-marketer" mindset shifts are functional experts and solo practitioners. Pay special attention to

Chapter 16, "If You ARE the Marketing Department, You've Got to Think Like One."

- Is this book both a "how-to guide" and a bit of an "inside-the-mind-of-a-marketer?"

  YES!   In my experience as a book publisher and an avid book reader, I've found that the best business books have it all — tips and strategies, principles and memorable stories, and honest insights about how things *really* work and what *truly* matters.

- Is this a good book to buy, recommend or pass along to a friend or colleague as a gift? Perhaps for someone who is trying to turn their side gig as a consultant into a full-time business, or someone who is trying to get noticed at work by sharing fresh perspectives and big ideas that generate return on investment (ROI)?

  YES!   I wish this book had existed for me when I was climbing the corporate ladder and learning through random fits of trial and error. With luck, this book can prevent a few headaches and inspire the greatness that's already inside its readers.

- If I enjoy the experience of reading this book and want to keep in touch afterward — maybe to hire Kate, hear her speak, chat with her on social media or have her publish MY book, can I do that?

  YES!   I sure hope you will! Please connect with me on LinkedIn, reach out via phone or email (see the Keep in Touch! section for all my vital details), and join our *Think Like a Marketer* community on Facebook. And if you have an idea for a "Think Like a ... " book inspired by the unique vantage points of another profession, I'd love to hear about it.

COMMUNICATE FOR MEANINGFUL CONNECTION

Communication is about connection. Connection is about people. And people matter.

Communication is about connection. Connection is about people. And people matter. Whatever industry you work in and whatever vital role you fill at your organization, I'm betting that the money only flows to your bottom line if human beings want your products or services — that communicating and connecting is everything, even though you might not think of marketing communications as a critical driver of your business. Take, for example, heavy equipment for construction. It would be easy for the leaders at a company like Caterpillar to think like "manufacturing people" or "finance people" or "engineering people" to the detriment of thinking like marketers. Many companies that sell big-ticket products and services to other businesses (i.e., companies that are business-to-business [B2B] in nature) falsely think that connecting at a personal level isn't necessary to their work. But they couldn't be more wrong. That's why Caterpillar is making waves with fun, edgy, modern marketing, through examples like their video that shows five machines (including excavators and telehandlers) playing a game of Jenga with 600-pound blocks. It's why their Edwards Demonstration and Learning Center — set on 720 acres of Illinois prairie with more dirt, machines and true "field experimentation" than you thought possible — is a destination for heavy-equipment operators and purchasers. You see, people love to play, and to be catered to, and to see or experience proof that the product or service they're considering is worth every penny. Be sure to check out Chapter 3 for a great deal more on this foundational principle of marketing. The proverbial (or actual) "test drives" and "free samples" are the gateway to sales, and they are possible — if you are creative enough in your thinking — in any industry and for any kind of customer.

People love to play, and to be catered to, and to see or experience proof that the product or service they're considering is worth every penny.

In addition to its role in driving sales, communications is valuable in and of itself. I happen to believe that when we're in business — any kind of business — we ought to be motivated every day by the way our business impacts people, lives, other organizations, economies and even ecosystems. Does your business have a communications strategy centering on connection, nurturing and making a difference? Would you keep executing that strategy if it was delighting customers but didn't seem measurably tied to short-term revenue? In Chapter 2, I'll talk about brand storytelling and challenge you to think about whether the way you communicate with your constituents (the style, the tone, the frequency, the channels) can and should be part of your overall business strategy and the story that you and the world tell about your organization.

Relationships — even in businesses as transient as consumer retail — begin with "hello," and how you say it matters.

Relationships — even in businesses as transient as consumer retail — begin with "hello," and how you say it matters.

Now that *we've* said hello, let's start exploring what it means to "think like a marketer" and how you can begin your mindset shift *today*.

01

WELCOME TO A NEW WAY OF THINKING ABOUT YOUR BUSINESS

Many business owners and leaders have a way of doing business that's about living in the frenzied current moment — chasing the next piece of revenue, getting through the next project, putting out the next proverbial fire or surviving the next people-problem that's bound to come up. It's a way of working that is so common as to be nearly universal and, for many of us, it's all we've ever known. But there's a better way.

It's time to think like a marketer! This book offers a fresh new approach to a more powerful, and lasting, way of doing business that involves a sometimes-subtle but always-impactful shift in mindset. If your company is like many others, you may currently be driven by a sales mindset. A sales mindset is not the same as a marketing mindset. Few companies are truly marketing driven, and I believe that's what's holding many people and organizations back. I'm excited to share with you the principles behind the practice and the insights behind the initiatives that have helped my clients eclipse the competition (and have allowed me to build a successful business in the process).

Most business owners and business leaders — regardless of their
company size or the industry they serve — tend to think of marketing
as a functional area or a cost center or, in only the very best of cases,
a strategic driver of business. But most of these professionals still
think of marketing in terms of departments, agencies, campaigns and
projects. Here's the truth that no one is speaking: What these leaders
need more than a great marketing director or a great marketing
agency is the right *marketing mindset*. It is the only way to achieve
profitable, sustainable growth.

**Here's the truth that no one is speaking: What these leaders
need more than a great marketing director or a great marketing
agency is the right *marketing mindset*. It is the only way to achieve
profitable, sustainable growth.**

Thank you for gifting me with a few hours of your valuable time
as you invest in reading this book. I think you'll find it full of fresh
ideas and insights to help you initiate new ways of thinking about
and operating in your business. We've all heard it said before: "You
be you, and I'll be me." And if you're an expert in a field other than
marketing — perhaps you're a management consultant or an IT
professional, a sought-after attorney or a chef who owns a popular
restaurant, a physician in private practice or a shopkeeper at
a specialty outdoor retailer — you don't have the time or inclination
to become a marketing expert, too! You just want to know the very
BEST insights from marketing experts, so you can apply them to your
career and your organization.

That's what this book is all about ... connecting you to big ideas
that are proven and based on the data, and helping you apply them
to whatever it is that you and your organization do. This book will

teach you to *think like a marketer* and, in turn, I hope it helps you to live like a king, so you can enjoy your work even more than you already do.

HOW SHOULD YOU READ THIS BOOK? READING WITH THE RIGHT MINDSET

You might be wondering: *Is this book for me?* Before you dig into the pages that follow, let me tell you a bit more about what this book will deliver, who it's for and how to approach the journey of reading.

This book is, at its simplest definition, for anyone looking to create more value for their customers or clients (or patients or donors or students or other stakeholders) and to capture more value through profit, paycheck or opportunity. Throughout the book, I'll attempt to keep you ahead of the curve by providing predictions. I'll also offer tips and tools, tie the stories and examples back to the *Think Like a Marketer* Principles, and challenge you to "ask yourself" questions that could spur breakthroughs, big and small.

This book is, at its simplest definition, for anyone looking to create more value for their customers or clients (or patients or donors or students or other stakeholders) and to capture more value through profit, paycheck or opportunity.

This book is for you if you are:

- **A business owner without a background in marketing.** Perhaps you're a consultant; a solopreneur; the founder of a small- to medium-sized company; a doctor, lawyer or accountant in private practice; or the owner of a brick-and-mortar retailer (wholly owned or a franchise). This book will be a great help to people who started their businesses as technical experts wanting to make their own rules and their own schedules — like IT professionals, finance/accounting pros, architects, doctors, lawyers or business consultants.

- **A business professional in a small- to mid-sized company** where budgets are tight, deadlines are tighter and everyone is an ad hoc marketer.

- **A business professional — whether a newcomer or veteran — in a Fortune 1000 company** where a breakthrough tip about connecting more meaningfully with customers could impact thousands or even millions of people, and where careers are made or broken one great, timely idea at a time.

- **A professional speaker, blogger or thought-leader** wanting to "put it all together" and connect to customers, clients, followers and audiences in new ways.

- **Non-profit professionals**, seeking to connect and create meaningful value for their constituents (customers, alumni, donors, community supporters, association members, etc.).

- **Marketers! (Especially young professionals just breaking into the field.)** If you've been working in marketing — on the business-to-consumer (B2C) or business-to-business (B2B) side — for less than a decade, you could probably use some been-there/done-that tips and words of wisdom about what really works.

  If you are a seasoned marketer, this book will be a refresher on strategies and stories that can help you breathe new life into your projects and perhaps change the way you think about the brands you have been entrusted with creating, growing and protecting. I hope it's also a good reminder of why you chose to become a marketer in the first place.

  Far from a simple "Marketing 101" for non-marketers, this book is a topical smorgasbord designed to feed the curiosities and satisfy the business needs that all business professionals (including marketers) ultimately crave.

- **Career relaunchers.** If you're coming back to the workforce after a time away, or are looking to break into something new — like an encore career after a first retirement — thinking like a marketer will provide you with a competitive edge in many ways.

WHAT DOES IT MEAN TO "THINK LIKE A MARKETER?" — 5 PRINCIPLES TO GUIDE YOU

There have been literally thousands of books written on effective leadership and none of them, including this one, has a magic formula for success. Marketing is not one-size-fits-all. But my career-long experiences working alongside business owners and business leaders at all levels have brought me to one truth that deserves to be shared and explored: Leaders who develop a marketing mindset — whose understanding of and dedication to the value of customer relationships and long-lasting brands always underpins their thinking and their decision-making — generate more value (financial and otherwise) for their organizations and their stakeholders. They also receive more satisfaction from their work than their marketing-blind counterparts. Marketing-minded business professionals get better results.

Marketing-minded business professionals get better results.

These 5 principles will guide you on the journey to becoming more marketing-minded. We'll explore these principles throughout the book, and I encourage you to expand my definitions into your own. Consider photocopying this list and putting it somewhere prominent in your office or your boardroom (or downloading a PDF of the 5 Principles at ThinkLikeAMarketerTheBook.com or at SilverTreeCommunications.com/5Principles). I promise it will inspire great things for you and your business.

Having a marketing mindset is not about becoming someone else or abandoning what makes you uniquely talented. It's about adding a dimension that helps you make better decisions and relate more effectively to others. By way of example, think about people who

THINK LIKE A MARKETER
5 PRINCIPLES TO GUIDE YOU

Thinking like a marketer requires that you:

1. Communicate for connection and meaning, not just to transact sales

2. Live and die by your customer insights

3. Market in a way that's strategy-religious and tactic-agnostic

4. Create cultures and processes that align with your brand

5. Do everything in service of maintaining a virtuous cycle of creating value for the customer while capturing value for you.

have "economist mindsets." They're the kind of people who, despite perhaps not being economists by trade, understand acutely how people (including customers, employees, children and others) respond to incentives. They don't stress out about walking away from a "sunk cost." Personally, "thinking like an economist" has helped me to make fruitful and customer-minded decisions for my business. It's also helped me let go of guilt and stress when I need to do the previously unthinkable, like cancel a (non-refundable) vacation I already paid $2,000 for (because I'm needed at home or the office). Mindset shifts can be life-changing ... they can be game-changing. They can also be good for the bottom line and your peace of mind.

So, what happens to careers and companies if professionals simply never learn to think like *marketers*? Many, many things can go wrong. Businesses shutter. Careers stagnate. Individual people suffer. I finally got the get-up-and-go to write this book because someone I knew was suffering the results of not thinking like a marketer. I was feeling sad and frustrated for him because he's brilliant and hard-working with unique experiences and insights, but was underemployed and unsure of the future. How did he get there? He wasn't thinking like a marketer. He was giving away all his insights and valuable content (as a blogger, consultant, speaker, webinar and workshop host, etc.), without putting price tags on his offerings or selling advertising or customer access to other brands who wanted to piggyback off his success and his large online following. I was heartbroken that despite all he was doing to create value for others, he had not yet found a way to capture value back for himself in return. That acute sense of heartbreak is what made me sit down and write the initial outline for this book.

Thinking like a marketer and running a successful business, department or program is about never losing sight of the yin/yang balance, and the never-ending virtuous cycle, of creating value and capturing value. You must do both. Create too little value for the customers, and there will be no value to capture in the end. Capture too little value for yourself or your business, and you'll quickly be out of resources (and energy) to create future value for your customers.

WILL "THINKING LIKE A MARKETER" HELP YOU WORK MORE EFFECTIVELY WITH ACTUAL MARKETERS?

Yes! It sure will. I have often said, "I'm not afraid to admit that I don't know what I don't know." With luck, you've said it, too. When it comes to catapulting your company or your career, though, you need to know a little something *about* what you don't know.

When it comes to marketing, you don't have to be the tactician — the copywriter, the graphic designer, the video editor, the media buyer, the market researcher, the analyst or the project manager. You don't even have to be the marketing strategist. If you work in a large organization, you likely have eminently qualified marketing leaders who have got you covered. But you do need to know when, how and why to assemble the strategists to help you arrive at collaborative new insights and the tacticians to execute on a thoughtful vision. When you think differently, you can sponsor or support projects differently. Thinking differently will allow you to change your organization or your product's story in a meaningful way.

Knowing when to reach out to a marketing consultant, a marketing agency or your marketing department is vital.

As a marketing consultant, my favorite clients are not the ones who are just like me. They are not the ones who do or who have done the same work I do. My favorite clients have taken the time to learn to shift their mindsets, even just slightly, so they know when to call me. Knowing when to reach out to a marketing consultant, a marketing agency or your marketing department is vital. In my business, these conversations often start like this (though perhaps not this formally):

> *"Kate, we need some tips. Our recent analysis of social media chatter has made it clear that the marketplace doesn't understand the primary use for our product. They think it's a 'nice to have' but haven't clued in to the way it can be a 'must have' for so many families and households. How can we rethink our story and articulate it in a more exciting and motivating way?"*

Or

> *"It's been four years since we last conducted a nationwide market research study to test the brand perception for our institution. We know that the attitudes, behaviors and strongly held beliefs of our prospective customers have probably changed in those four years.*

But we'd only be guessing if we were to build a new marketing plan based on those changes without actually going out and getting the data. We think it's time to repeat the research before sales begin to slip."

Or

"We're so excited! We're just a few months away from introducing our new product, and it's time to design the packaging and the advertising. We feel 90% confident we know who our target customer is and what she cares about. But we're not so foolish as to go to market without testing some of those assumptions. Can you help?"

These leaders — whether they're embarking on a long-term, big-budget project or just refreshing a four-page sales brochure — are "thinking like marketers." Think-like-a-marketer leaders plus actual professional marketers are a great combination. Together, they can change so much — in such powerful ways — for their businesses. Just remember, though ... developing a marketing mindset requires continued and even renewed respect and trust in your marketers (whether they're in-house marketers or agencies/consultants). It requires that your marketing team has a seat at the leadership and decision-making table. Business leaders and owners who master a marketing mindset don't eliminate the need for great marketers — they create opportunities to see eye-to-eye with marketers, to move major initiatives forward in more effective ways and to have their own marketing-minded epiphanies.

Business leaders and owners who master a marketing mindset
don't eliminate the need for great marketers — they create
opportunities to see eye-to-eye with marketers, to move major
initiatives forward in more effective ways and to have their own
marketing-minded epiphanies.

WHAT DO YOU WANT TO BE KNOWN FOR?
A PRIMER IN BEING MEANINGFULLY DIFFERENT

Some business professionals think that success in marketing is about
being better — having higher-quality products and services for
a better price. Others will argue it's about being different — offering
a product or service you can't get anywhere else. I think the "better
vs. different" camps are both partially right, and this topic is of great
interest to me. I built my own marketing practice on a brand promise
of *Be Meaningfully Different*™. Every day, we help clients express
their points of difference through powerful stories and well-targeted
communications. But even the most *different* kind of different can be
meaningless. I'm finishing this book during the summer — a season
when wine and cheese can be the perfect way to start an afternoon.
I live in Wisconsin, where the grocery stores have 2-3 aisles just for
cheese, and I'd argue that some cheeses are different and others are
meaningfully different. Take, for example, Smoky Swiss & Cheddar,
a blend that's savory and sweet, sharp and mellow — a cheese that
melts perfectly on a salmon burger or that makes you go "mmm"
on a cracker. In the very same "Cheese Castle" that can sell you
that Smoky Swiss & Cheddar (which I would argue is meaningfully
different from your run-of-the-mill Colby Jack) is Dairy Fudge, or
chocolate cheese. Cheese and chocolate; brown cheese. It's *different*
alright. But is it meaningful? Building a brand that can stand the test

of time and that will generate appreciable revenue is all about being *"meaningfully* different."

Ask yourself: *Is our company meaningfully different? Are our products differentiated from the competition and do they offer a meaningful feature or benefit to the marketplace?* If your answer is a little ho-hum, this is the place to do some serious brainstorming about what could make your company and/or your products and services more different, more meaningful or both. Sometimes a minor tweak can make a major difference.

Who Decides What You Stand For?

The customer does. In the end, the marketplace owns your brand. They (not you) decide whether you're prestigious or pedestrian, whether your product is worth $5 or $45 (or your consulting time is worth $75 an hour or $250 an hour), and whether what you do for them is so valuable that they ought to tell their friends or colleagues about it.

In the end, the marketplace owns your brand. They (not you) decide whether you're prestigious or pedestrian, whether your product is worth $5 or $45 (or your consulting time is worth $75 an hour or $250 an hour), and whether what you do for them is so valuable that they ought to tell their friends or colleagues about it.

There is much you can do to influence the attitudes, behaviors and buying decisions of your customers — and I hope you pick up a lot of those ideas in this book — but the customer ultimately supports you, shops with you and sings your praises, or she rolls her eyes, closes her wallet and writes negative online reviews.

Let me share a personal (and admittedly nostalgic and folksy) story about how I, as a customer, have repeatedly decided that car dealership brands aren't meaningful "brands" to me at all. Longer ago than I can remember (and probably long before I could drive a car), my grandma taught me to demand that car dealerships take the dealer-branded bumper sticker off my new car if they weren't going to pay me a monthly fee for the advertising I'd be doing by driving around with their name on my car. (She was sassy like that and smart, too!) The reason such a fussy demand made good sense (and yes, I've done it multiple times, even when the sticker had already been applied to the bumper and then needed to be carefully removed) is because never in my life has a car dealership created a meaningful relationship or custom-built a car (i.e., unique product) for me that changed my life. They wheedle and push, charge too much for the product and the ongoing service, waste my time, and treat me like they can't believe that my husband (who's usually busy checking email from his phone in the corner of the showroom while I'm making a major purchase), isn't absolutely necessary to my decision to buy myself a car. So far, no car dealership has ever demonstrated *meaningful difference* to me — two dealerships selling Audis are interchangeable, as are two dealerships selling Nissans or Subarus. If they have the car I want on the lot and can give me the price I'm willing to pay, they're my "dealer of the moment." There's absolutely no guarantee I'll be back to make a second purchase from them. (In fact, I've never bought more than one car from the same auto dealership.)

There are, of course, auto dealerships offering meaningful difference — trusted relationships, unique financing options, custom cars. I've just never visited one. It's worth noting that new services, where I can buy a car online and have it delivered to my driveway, may entirely disrupt the age-old dilemma regarding how one car dealership or salesperson differentiates from the others. I, for one, am curious to see how this industry evolves.

Could car dealerships be like Panera, where — for telecommuters and entrepreneurs, sales people and career networkers — it's not just about the food (though their healthy menu is, indeed, meaningfully different)? At Panera, it's about connection and community. It's a restaurant where you can spend hours on the free wifi and only buy a cup of coffee or a muffin. Could car dealers do that, going beyond the cars to stand for something bigger? Could you?

Maybe the very nature of running a car dealership makes it diffi-cult to be buzz-worthy in a way that's anything other than hokey. ("Come turn this key at our customer-appreciation event to see if you won a free TV!") But the good news is that other brands (including yours (!) ... even if you run a car dealership!) have every opportunity to earn the affection of their customers and clients — people who would freely OFFER to tell their Instagram followers about you, write you a LinkedIn recommendation or a review or testimonial for your services or company, share your Facebook post, put your branded sticker on the back of their laptop or cell phone, or wear your t-shirt. (All of these social-sharing and brand-advocacy behaviors are the modern-day equivalents of putting a bumper sticker on your car.)

By way of ultra-timely example, I wrote this chapter of my book while sitting in the crow's nest on a Holland America Line (HAL) cruise ship (and I'd gladly tell you that HAL has taken us to Alaska and the Caribbean for adventures we loved and that the amenities and services were excellent in relation to the price we paid). I'm typing from a Microsoft Surface (in my humble opinion, the traveling professional's best option when considering a laptop or tablet for business), and have an "Ask Me About My Book" sticker on the back side of my Surface (a sticker that has triggered fun conversations on airplanes and in boardrooms, and a sticker that contains a tiny plug for CathyFyock.com (the internet home for my book coach). The irony is not lost on me — that people pay me to help promote their products and services, and yet there are many products and services I gladly promote for free. Why do I do so? Because, in my life and work, those brands have demonstrated meaningful difference to me.

What are you doing in your business to hardwire this kind of loyalty among your customers, clients, fans, followers, influencers or supporters?

The Brands and Businesses I Can't Stop Talking About

We're all "fans" and promoters of products, services, companies, charities, social organizations and professional associations. Choose a random brand by looking around your house or office right now. Maybe you stopped at the Room Essentials desk fan from Target or the Apple iPhone in your hand or the church you attend, which sent an inspirational newsletter to you. Ask yourself: "On a scale of 0 to 10, with 10 being 'extremely likely' and 0 being 'not at all likely,' how likely are you to recommend that brand to a friend?" If you answered a 9 or 10, you are a promoter of that brand. A 7 or 8 and you're considered a "passive" (you're not driving the growth of the brand but not hurting it either). If you answered between a 0 and a 6, you're a brand detractor. This simple, but powerful question, is what's called a Net Promoter Score® measurement (a concept developed by Bain & Company), and is a proven leading indicator of future performance and business health for companies and brands in every sector.

So, if you're an avid fan — a "promoter," if you will — of a brand, what does it take for that brand to earn that kind of loyalty from you? I suggest giving it some deep thought and then figuring out how your own company can engender that same kind of loyalty. Below are some of the brands and businesses that I can't stop talking about, and that I'd prefer not to imagine my life without. Let me tell you why. (Could these rave reviews and enthusiastic words be said about *your* brand?)

- **Amazon**

  At the risk of pointing out the obvious, no one has mastered the art of convenience like they have. I can order products from any device with one click. I never have to dig out a credit card. If I use *their* credit card, I earn points that I can spend like cash. Almost everything I buy ships for free. They seem to carry just about anything I could want. Their book business (including their print-on-demand book printing service, CreateSpace, their Kindle Direct Publishing platform and their ACX audiobook exchange) is vital to my own business. Their reviews help guide my purchases. Returns are easy to make. And since Amazon opened 1.5 million square feet of warehouse space here in my hometown of Kenosha, WI, I can sometimes literally order a product at breakfast time and have it on my porch before dinner. (No kidding.)

- **Chicos**

  Say what you will about it being the "place women over 40 shop for clothes" — it's true and I love them. (And yes, I'm over 40!) They've come up with a sizing system that makes women of all sizes feel normal (not too skinny nor too fat). They run fantastic sales online and in their brick-and-mortar stores. Their clothes are classy and beautiful, and worth every penny because they never fade or lose their shape. And they always carry several pieces in related color palettes, so it's easy to build coordinated ensembles. They also train their associates to act like personal shoppers when you head to the fitting rooms, so they bring you everything you could possibly need. You never leave empty handed or feeling anything less than beautiful and well outfitted.

- **Holland America Line**

I'm still relatively new to the seafaring lifestyle, with my upcoming cruise set to be just my fourth. And while Disney Cruise Line surely sets the bar for experience and magic, a Disney cruise isn't always within reach financially. So I've become loyal to and enthusiastic about Holland America Line (HAL) because they make vacationing so easy. Every ship has a similar layout, so I feel "at home" as soon as I board; they have upscale and exclusive perks like a thermal spa you need to experience to believe. They go the extra mile to take care of guests with food allergies. They run outstanding "private sales" for repeat cruisers with prices that are too good to pass up and they enjoy celebrating alongside their guests. We recently attended a wedding on board a HAL ship, and cakes and rose petals and special well-wishes for the happy couple abounded at every unexpected turn, even though none of those perks were planned or paid for.

- **Lavender Hill Massage**

Who doesn't love a great massage? But not all massages are created equal. There are so many things I love about Erica at Lavender Hill Massage in Pleasant Prairie, WI. She understands how to give a "light touch" massage for sensitive clients, which leaves you relaxed and unknotted without causing bruises or being too delicate to be worthwhile. And she has every detail of the experience accounted for — from the hot steamy towel when you're finished (so you can use it to clear your sinuses after lying face-down for so long!), to the breath mints, tissues and even a cold bottle of water for the road.

- **Logitech**

  They make the best computer peripherals — affordable, long-lasting and often even stylish. I'm particularly enamored with their R800 Laser Presentation Remote (i.e., PowerPoint clicker), which has a rubber coating and ergonomic design that fits my hand perfectly, a built-in laser pointer, a digital countdown clock, and the ability to silently vibrate in my hand when I've only got a few minutes left to finish my presentation. It's a tool that makes me more effective at work, which makes me grateful, and *that* makes me a talkative recommender of the product.

- **Magnolia & Vine by Angel**

  If you haven't experienced this jewelry for yourself or someone you love, it's time. Gorgeous but affordable jewelry that you "design yourself" by changing out the interchangeable "snaps" to turn one necklace, one bracelet or one pair of earrings into dozens of designs. Their jewelry makes me look put together and coordinated. I attract compliments every time I wear it, and it is made without nickel, so it's safe for my skin. They also make traveling/packing so easy (I just fill up a little bag full of "snaps" that match my outfits, and I'm good to go!). Magnolia & Vine is sold through a network of marketers, and I get my jewelry from my friend Angel, who is a master of consultative selling and helps me make smart purchases worth celebrating.

- **Microsoft Surface**

  When it comes to laptop computers and tablets for business, I feel like I've tried them all. I've toted around the heavy, full-sized laptops that hurt my shoulders and neck, and I've worked on little "netbooks" that were easy to transport but left much to be desired in terms of the keyboard and overall performance. Then I discovered the Microsoft Surface, which has changed how I work, especially in airplanes and hotel rooms. It's light, versatile, powerful, a tablet and laptop in one, and comes fully loaded with all the Microsoft Office software I need to be productive. I've owned two of them so far and will be a customer for life. Yes, every time I show it to someone new, I have to pull it apart and pop it back together to demonstrate the unique and utterly cool magnetic "click-together" way that the keyboard and screen are joined (a truly meaningful difference that has been so well marketed in television commercials and online videos). The Surface is premium priced for a premium product.

- **Nanoglutathione by Nanoceutical Solutions**

This breakthrough supplement has changed my life by improving my health in many ways. And getting this precious liquid to my house and into my bloodstream could not be easier, thanks to outstanding distribution and customer care. The sleek blue bottles are shipped to my home every 30 days, but it takes a simple email to trigger a delay if I'm not in need of any more, and the customer service team is anything but nameless and faceless. I have real relationships with people who I know by name, and when I offered to produce videos and write testimonials for this product, which has helped put my interstitial cystitis (a painful bladder disease) into remission and improved my sleep, the marketing team at Nanoceutical Solutions was generous in offering me "insider" discounts for being a loyal advocate for their products. Interested in learning more? Check out my video review of Nanoglutathione on YouTube.

- **National Speakers Association**

  As you'll learn in the chapter about networking, I'm notorious for flitting in and out of professional associations, based on my needs and my budget. Conferences and associations have always felt like giant conglomerations of strangers who have something in common but can't quite connect. Imagine my surprise when I got to know the people of the National Speakers Association (NSA). With state and local chapters to make the big group feel like friends, the organization is full of opportunity and brimming with generous members willing to share insights and time. At my first national conference in 2018 (Influence18 in Dallas), I received special seating at general sessions because I was a "VIP" (a first-time attendee), was assigned an incredible mentor to be my "buddy" for the week (she even came to hear me speak) and was treated like a worthy colleague when I took the stage. NSA really *gets it* when it comes to *Think Like a Marketer* Principle #4 — "Create cultures and processes that align with your brand."

- **OlovesM**

  This quirky and awesome company makes environmentally friendly tote bags and other products using yoga mats and fabric over-runs. I've been carrying my red and white tote for more years than I can remember and it still looks brand new. Why I love these products? They're fun and stylish; they make use of products that were going to end up in a landfill; they're family-owned; you can wipe off the dirt with a damp cloth and your tote or purse or wallet looks good as new; the straps and zippers can take a beating; and they're more spacious than they look. OlovesM is also a brand with a story — about yoga, about creativity, about sustainability and about a love story.

- **PopSockets**

  If you don't have a PopSocket attached to your phone, what are
  you waiting for? I have carpal tunnel (which is burning like fire
  as I write this) but having a "knob" on the back of my iPhone
  makes it easier to hold while working and socializing, and it lets
  me achieve a more flattering angle for selfies, as well as serves
  as a totally awesome "kickstand" to hold the phone if I want to
  watch a video. As a marketer, I also love that PopSockets come
  in seemingly limitless designs to suit any style and can even
  be custom branded. Universities and other institutions are
  imprinting their logos on PopSockets and delighting stakeholders
  while turning them into walking billboards. (Remember the car
  dealership bumper sticker? Yep. This is the modern-day version,
  and no one is resisting. I recently gave a Northeastern University
  PopSocket to a dear friend; despite her not having an affiliation with the University, she immediately and enthusiastically
  attached it to her phone.)

- **Southwest Airlines**

  What's not to love? Affordable airfare, friendly and fun staff,
  comfortable accommodations, clean planes, on-time departures,
  outstanding customer service, a great mobile app and a company
  that hasn't had a layoff in its history. They've successfully avoided
  the "requirement" and expense of being listed on sites like
  Expedia because they know their customers are loyal enough
  to come straight to Southwest.com for their travel planning. At
  Southwest, I have been sung to, told jokes, complimented and
  pampered. The week before completing this book manuscript,
  I had the opportunity to meet CEO Gary Kelly, who delivered an
  inspiring talk on "good old-fashioned civility" and then gave a

$100 Southwest gift card to everyone in the audience. Seriously. Why would you fly with anyone else?

- **Tieks**

At the risk of attracting criticism for my penchant for expensive footwear, I just have to sing the praises of Tieks, the company that reinvented the ballet flat with Italian leather shoes that are as beautiful as they are comfortable. Aside from being a well-made shoe, Tieks is a well-made brand. Over the years, they have sent me hand-written notes for my birthday, have gotten a member of the C-suite to jump on a live web chat to help me surprise a colleague with a discounted pair of shoes, and more. They understand that fashionistas don't just want an option for yellow shoes but rather, they need three *different shades* of yellow. They've mastered the art of offering exclusivity without fussiness by having a product that regularly sells out but then ensuring I'm just one website click away from getting on the mailing list to be notified when that perfect shade is available in my size. Their packaging is keep-worthy and among the only mailbox delivery that could make me squeal. Each gorgeous shoebox is adorned with a sparkly flowered headband. And their gift cards? Yep, they come in a tiny "shoebox" with a tiny flower. No gift card has ever felt like a "gift-opening" experience before or since.

- **WunderList**

I'm ending my list of brands I love by sharing a mobile app that's for (you guessed it) making lists. I can't overstate how this app has improved my life. My husband and I use it for our shared grocery list. My handyman and I use it for our shared project list. I use it for vacation packing, holiday planning and every-thing you can imagine. What makes this the best "list app?" So many things. Social sharing, the little "chime" that sounds when you complete an item (it makes you feel so accomplished!), the email notifications when your husband finishes something on his honey-do list, the ability to set deadlines and sub-tasks as well as to upload images into the list so "buy eyeliner" will have a photo of the correct brand. Not to mention, the ability to undo items on a list so you can repopulate next week's grocery list or next month's vacation packing list. Sometimes, the best brands are the ones that solve a problem you didn't know could be so perfectly solvable.

As you can see from my list of current favorite brands, there are many qualities — from social responsibility to convenient distribution to superior product quality — that create a "meaningful difference" for customers. Meaningful difference is what wins you new business in the first place, and it's also what inspires repeat business, larger sales and new referrals. Your business offerings might be cool or valuable enough to a customer for them to try you *once*, but then what? Difference by itself isn't enough; even the most fleeting fads offer difference. Meaningful difference, on the other hand, is sustainable. True meaning can also keep the competitors at bay. Eventually, the competition might try to copy your difference, but if you've hardwired (into your business and the way you deliver your products and services) multiple ways to keep customers loyal, you stand a stronger chance of being viable for the long run. Ask yourself whether you can deliver your awesome product or its attractive price or its "fanatical customer service" (a brand promise from the good people at Rackspace) in a way that's incredibly difficult to clone.

Now let's turn the page and talk about how to *articulate* your meaningful difference. What do you and your company want to be known for? Perhaps you're a consultant who wants to be known as "the person who wrote the book on (insert expertise)" or the one who delivers your professional services in an innovative way.

Or maybe you represent a shop that wants to be *the* place to go for the best apparel and gear for outdoor activities because your sales team provides second-to-none consultation about products that will improve customer performance, keep them dry and warm in the winter, and help them to build amazing memories during their outdoor adventures. Whatever you want to be known for, there are thoughtful ways to take that clarity and strategy to drive everything about the way you do business, starting with the story you tell to the marketplace.

02

HAVE A GREAT STORY AND KNOW HOW TO TELL IT

STRATEGIC STORYTELLING

Most companies advertise to or otherwise communicate with the people they'd like to turn into customers. Many are working hard and spending even harder to share those messages. But few companies know how to tell a compelling story, and some don't even know what their story is. Communicating generic messages like "Sale ends Friday" simply won't work unless your product is such a standout and so meaningfully different that your customers are clamoring to have one.

Yesterday, I heard the ice cream truck driving through the neighborhood, with calliope music blaring in its Pied-Piper attempt to lure sugar-loving children from their homes and backyards. That guy behind the wheel doesn't even *have* to tell a story — because he's the only merchant offering individually wrapped ice cream treats at the foot of our driveways. Hot, hungry children and tired parents who are counting the days until school starts again will buy, repeatedly and indiscriminately.

But if you're like most business leaders, your product or service has stiff competition. You have to find a way to help people understand your value and your difference. Are you the low-cost leader with industry-best operational efficiency, like a Wal-Mart? The leader in product excellence, like Nike? Or the stand-out provider of customer intimacy, like Nordstrom?

If you're like most business leaders, your product or service has stiff competition. You have to find a way to help people understand your value and your difference.

At the risk of using too many metaphors while making a simple point, I have found that many business professionals can't see the forest for the trees. They are so busy managing the demanding day-to-day operations of their organizations — from motivating their people to sourcing their materials to managing the finances — that they don't take the time to examine what drives the customer's buying behaviors, what the competition is up to, and what will move the dial in terms of revenue. That's where strategic storytelling comes in. With a compelling and memorable story — that is your signature and "ownable" by your brand — you can begin to pull away from the competition. Your products and services will sell in the short term, and your company brand will survive in the long-run.

Not long ago, I saw a commercial for a cancer program at an area hospital. Cancer treatment is big business in the United States, and — while it's uncomfortable to even talk about profiting from illness and fear — cancer centers must find a way to convince the public that they are the only choice for innovative treatment options. In this particular commercial, clips of people playing backyard soccer with their kids and a woman getting a piggyback ride from her husband in the park were shown. They told a story about happy, healthy people living the kinds of lives we can relate to and admire, and then they tell us all those moments "began with a second opinion" at their facility. While I can't speak to their bedside manner, technology or patient outcomes, I can tell you that this storytelling approach in their marketing is a strong one. As the viewer — and someone who is well aware that there are many, many oncology practices available in a 50-mile radius — I am left with a clear message: "If I have cancer or a loved one has cancer, and the future seems unsure, I have to get a second opinion from this place." The commercial doesn't waste any of its valuable 30 seconds talking about generic, universal things like "integrated care" or "world-class doctors." Instead, it focuses relentlessly on its story.

Every brand can have a compelling story — whether you're selling iPods or ice cream or integrated cancer care. And stories matter.

Perhaps it was inevitable that I would commit my career to storytelling. As a student, I was fascinated with mythologies — Greek, Roman, Hebrew, American, religious and secular. I even began naming my dogs after goddesses (I have had Shelties named Calypso, Luna and Chloe). The timeless nature of our mythologies is a strong reminder that stories matter. They help to explain the world. They make our existence relevant, safe, inviting, romantic or meaningful. As business professionals, we too have an opportunity to explain and to inspire. So, whether you're trying to change the world or raise your stock price (or both), the perfect place to start is with a story that sticks.

DISCOVERING AND ARTICULATING YOUR STORY

Hard as it might be to believe, not every business owner or leader knows their company's story. Many companies, in fact, have never familiarized themselves with their story, much less articulated it. They are busy selling products, taking orders, etc. — they've never put a stake into the ground about who they are, what they stand for or what makes them different. Savvy companies have written this down on paper. A brand story platform contains the following:

- A core story of several paragraphs or even pages

- Positioning language in various lengths and styles that might start with "We are the company that ... " or "We help this kind of customer achieve this kind of result"

- Suggested headlines and pull-quotes (bite-sized, powerful language that can be translated into elevator speeches or marketing messages)

- A vocabulary list of words and phrases you want to associate with your brand, and even a list of rules about words and phrases you and your team will *never* use when telling your story

- Guiding principles about the story you want to convey, the people and organizations you want to communicate with, the tone you want to strike, the personality you want to build, and the results you want to achieve

- Specific plans for how to share vital bits of your story — regularly and powerfully — on social media to spur sales, attract new customers and earn loyalty. Consider being proactively clear about whether your brand personality or voice on social media will be different from the voice you use elsewhere. Will it be more personal, casual, humorous, hip?

Story is strategy. Does your organization have a clear story that goes beyond what's currently on your website, and is it written down somewhere in a business document? It has been my experience that the companies that have a solid brand story platform — including solo practitioners like speakers, consultants, private practice physicians and attorneys — are companies that are better equipped to pivot during times of change. They are better steeled against distractions that don't align with their brand, they are more likely to attract and retain customers, and are more efficient in their operations. I'd argue that every organization ought to do the work of developing a brand platform document and that companies with lots of spokespeople (i.e., more than 10 employees) MUST have a brand platform document. It becomes a playbook and a compass.

Story is strategy. Does your organization have a clear story that goes beyond what's currently on your website, and is it written down somewhere in a business document?

Writing a brand story isn't as easy as writing up a first draft in answer to the bulleted items above. Arriving at those words requires making major decisions (and tradeoffs) and can take days, weeks or months to achieve. But the work is worth it. Once a company clarifies its story, it has many options for the ways and places in which to share the story. Marketing tactics are "megaphones" for the story, and bits and pieces of it can be shared on websites and in videos, through your staff, your advertising, your social media and your public relations efforts.

So, how can you arrive at a solid and comprehensive brand story platform to guide you? It's ultimately about deep, open-minded conversations. Work with a business storytelling expert (typically a brand marketer who is a great writer) or with a colleague on your team to talk through all the elements of the story. I recently had these conversations with Mimi Vold, the founder of Vold Inc., a premier advisory firm for growth-stage companies. Through our conversations, we discovered that while she thought she served one market at the time she'd partnered with me, she ended up being ideal for another. She had been using words and phrases to describe herself and her work that weren't quite right, and that weren't opening the right conversations or closing the big deals. It took hours and hours — of her own thinking and writing, of homework assignments, of us talking together and of me finally assembling these conversations and insights into a brand story platform — to get where she is today, which is in the right place with clear messages that appeal to a marketplace ready and willing to hire her. (Her unofficial but unequivocal tagline? "Scaling Experts, Valuation Accelerators.")

Developing a brand story is a thinking exercise first, a decision-making exercise second, and writing exercise third.

Developing a brand story is a thinking exercise first, a decision-making exercise second, and writing exercise third.

SOME INSIDER TIPS ON BRAND STORYTELLING

Timing matters: Should you work on your story now or later? Can startups afford to develop a brand story platform, and do they even know who they are just yet? I'd argue that if you don't know who you are and who you want to serve right this moment (knowing that your focus might change over time), you have no business being in business just yet.

So many companies in desperate need of brand storytelling assistance don't call me (or other storytelling consultants) until their sales are slumping and they are suffering. They finally feel enough pain to admit the marketplace doesn't know what makes them different. Suddenly, five years or 15 years or 50 years into their organizational history, they're finally getting around to "getting their story straight." When they do, remarkable changes can happen.

Smart companies, of course, call us before they open their doors, sometimes before they name their companies, before they have a logo, or before they launch their new brands, products or services. It costs less, and it hurts less upfront. This vital work at the startup phase is both marketing and business consulting in one, and it can help founders and leaders get laser focused early in the game.

Every company should have a detailed version of their story, but I'm a strong believer that distilling your meaningful difference into just a few words is vital. Developing a tagline or a brand promise helps you get to the heart of what you do, how you do it differently and who you do it for.

The power of brevity: Every company should have a detailed version of their story, but I'm a strong believer that distilling your meaningful difference into just a few words is vital. Developing a tagline or a brand promise helps you get to the heart of what you do, how you do it differently and who you do it for. Take, for example, Walgreens and the tagline they recently retired: "At the Corner of Happy and Healthy." This tagline told their entire story in a few simple words. Consumers who know the Walgreens brand well are those who know that the company has a real estate strategy as well as a product strategy. It involves being located on street corners, an architecture strategy of putting the front door on the corner of the building, and offering a product and service selection in two categories — those that aim to make customers healthier (prescription and over-the-counter medications, supplements and hygiene products) and those that aim to make customers happier (greeting cards and makeup, snacks and candies and gifts). Walgreens is also a great example that taglines can, do and must change over time. In direct reaction to emerging rivals — like Amazon, which is entering the pharmacy distribution business — Walgreens introduced its new tagline, "Trusted Since 1901," to remind the marketplace that their competitors, particularly those in the ecommerce space, don't have the heritage, experience or trusted following that Walgreens does.

Taglines and brand promises also help customers connect with you. But they should be more than a slogan. To stand the test of time and to mean something to the customer, they must be *ownable* by your company. The former Walgreens tagline could have been used by their competitors, but the "corner" concept applied in an ownable way. And take for example the evolution of the tagline at my MBA alma mater. For a period of time, they used "Heads of Business Head the Class" to emphasize the fact that the faculty are business leaders at area companies. But because not all faculty members were "heads" (i.e., founders, CEOs, etc.), the tagline was abandoned over concerns that it was an over-promise. While I was a student in the program, the tagline was "Learn from Experience" — a nod to the experience of the faculty, the average 13 years of professional experience of the students and the hands-on, experiential learning model itself. This tagline resonated with incoming students and with current students. But it left out the alumni, who — once they'd graduated — were no longer part of that process/experience. So, the tagline was eventually changed to speak to the results — no longer about the *how*, but about the *who* and the *what*. The new tagline, "Broad Thinkers,

Strong Leaders," is a bold promise about what students and alumni become as a result of the broad general management curriculum. It's an aspirational idea for prospective students, a point of pride for current students and a proof point for alumni. These four words speak to every stakeholder.

Stories can reveal new insights and drive business decisions: I happen to think that brand stories are so much more than "marketing." In finding your story, you can often find areas of new focus and investment for your organization, like when I worked with a global pharmaceutical and medical device company to develop a brand story and we discovered, in the process, that their million-dollar equipment wasn't all that different from the competitor's offerings, but that the wrap-around and support services (including second-to-none technical staff) were what made their products the clear choice for hospitals and laboratories. Suddenly, it was apparent that those staff and the service contracts offered to customers needed attention and investment. The competitive edge went beyond the equipment itself.

I happen to think that brand stories are so much more than "marketing." In finding your story, you can often find areas of new focus and investment for your organization.

Similarly, stories can and should drive business decisions in appreciable ways for customers, like when CVS Health made the controversial decision in 2015 to stop selling cigarettes and tobacco, as a way to "put its money where its mouth is" when it comes to its commitment to the health of its customers. Or the example of the medical university where I once worked, Rosalind Franklin University of Medicine and Science, using its brand story and strategy — Life in Discovery® — to drive decisions about what academic programs to fund and start, what connections to make in the community and what research to pursue.

What changes, shifts or sacrifices are you willing to make in service to your brand story?

UNDERSTANDING YOUR STORY CAN ALSO HELP YOU UNDERSTAND WHICH CUSTOMERS TO TARGET

Without a clear story, you could be running the wrong business and/or serving the wrong customers.

In developing your brand story, you may find that you'll have a big "a-ha" about who you want to serve. When I first wrote the web copy and marketing copy for Silver Tree, I thought I wanted to work only with CEOs, so we positioned ourselves as being focused on CEO-to-CEO relationships. And while I still work with a great many CEOs, my "CEO-to-CEO" story was keeping me from attracting business from larger corporations, where CEOs don't make the hiring decisions about marketing consultants.

I was going after the wrong market (i.e., small and medium-sized businesses only) because I had whipped up some web copy without completing the full exercise of developing a core story, making tough decisions about the vocabulary we'd use, and getting granular about identifying the difference that was *meaningful* in addition to just being different for the sake of difference. I was doing the right kind of work, but was sometimes going after the wrong relationship when I started the company. That was a big discovery for me when I took the time to recraft my story based on where I wanted to be and how my work made me feel. Perhaps this was related to a sort of arrogance. I wanted to work with CEOs because it sounded important but, at the end of the day, I do my best work when I'm working with the VP of marketing, the head of product innovation or the director of sales, for example. (And, interestingly, fancy as it sounds to work with the founder or CEO, sometimes he or she was running a tiny business that couldn't afford me or didn't truly value me.)

If you're a small business owner or solopreneur, it's especially important to ask yourself this question during your story development phase: "What work depletes me versus what work energizes me?" Try to think about this when you get off a call with a client or when you deliver a project. Are you running around the office because you're excited that it's over? Or are you running around the office excited that you delivered such a cool project for such cool people and you hope they hire you again? There's a real difference. The exact same kind of work delivered to the right vs. the wrong customer can leave you feeling quite different. Be in business for the right customer, and let your story guide you in choosing.

Be in business for the right customer, and let your story guide you in choosing.

After my discovery about my exhaustion with the CEOs of poorly funded small businesses and my need and desire to move "up stream," as it were, I put a Post-It on the wall next to my computer. It said: "I am not your mom-and-pop shop's little marketing intern." Every time I got a call or an email asking for my help with a project clearly too junior for my organization, I looked at that piece of paper and kindly said, "No, thank you." Knowing which clients to choose and which to reject is a mindset — it's about getting clear. If you were really honest, what would *your* Post-It say (about your best customers, your best products, your clear difference or what you want to be known for)? How might that Post-It change your business?

As for who we *do* serve at Silver Tree (in our marketing consulting practice and in our book publishing business), our story continually drives those customer decisions. We are driven by dreams and personalities; by human health and vitality; by the desire to know more and do better and to leave an impression on the lives of those around us. Our clarity about that purpose and story helps us identify who to work with. It's why we work with healthcare organizations and universities, and motivational speakers and authors who have powerful messages. We work with charities that improve lives and communities and with other companies doing admirable work to help make people stronger and the world a better place in which to live.

Here's another great exercise to try when clarifying your brand story. Make a list of items about your business in which every sentence starts with "We don't" or "We won't." Perhaps you don't charge retainers. Or you don't hassle customers about product returns. Or you won't take on business that hurts the environment. Do your customers, partners and key stakeholders know the details about what you *don't* do and where you draw lines in the sand? If they're unclear about these guidelines, consider what it might mean to your story if you were upfront and unapologetic about these points of difference (that is, of course, if they are *meaningfully* different).

DETAILS MATTER

Once you've gotten clear on your meaningful difference and the way you'll articulate it through your story, it's important to be mindful of the details. Remember that not all storytelling takes place through words. When we announced the name change at Rosalind Franklin University, the story about DNA pioneer Dr. Franklin — for whom the institution was being renamed — was told through the details as well, like the flowers in test tubes on the cocktail tables at the reception (a nod to the pursuit of science), and the selection of the people we brought on stage to honor her (like modern female pioneers, such as Dr. Sally Ride, America's first woman in space). No matter what kind of business you're in, pieces of your brand story can be told through the creative details, like the right music (Chipotle is known for their loud, modern music in the dining room) or an unforgettable scent (Harborside Inn in Boston smells like green tea and makes guests feel a sense of "ahhh" the moment they step into the lobby).

Be thinking, as well, about how business stories contain anchors and focal points. At Rosalind Franklin University, the unsung nature of their namesake, as well as her pioneering discoveries, are an anchor. The marketing team found various ways to connect the stories of current students and faculty to Dr. Franklin's own life and work (like when our announcement video featured an MD student saying, "I'm the first person in my family to go to medical school. So, when you think about it, I'm a pioneer too.").

Small businesses (and large ones!) can have personalities and cute, or even quirky, personas. Ask my clients, and they're likely to remember that our dogs (who are in our offices every day) are in our marketing videos and inspired our blog name (Brand's Best Friend). Our furry friends make us smile around here, and we like to make our clients smile too. Incidentally, if you've never discovered that the 404/page-not-found error on the Amazon website features rotating images and stories about dogs owned by Amazon employees, be sure to go check it out. Quirk is different; personality is endearing; endeared customers are more loyal.

Don't forget the details. A few weeks ago, I had a makeover at
a high-end cosmetics shop in Highland Park, IL, called CosBar. At
the beginning of my two-hour visit, I fell in love with a perfume and
proceeded to periodically wiggle in front of my nose the scented
cardboard strip. *Mmmm.* Floral and light. As I was checking out and
buying some bronzer, I asked my beauty consultant, Sheena, how
much the perfume cost. The price tag, as it turned out, was way out
of my comfort zone, so when I told her I'd pass, she just nodded
and smiled and rang me up. As I was taking my debit card from my
purse, she casually stepped out from behind the cash register and
walked over to the perfume counter, picking up the bottle I'd liked so
much and spritzing the fragrance all over the tissue paper in my bag.
She didn't say a word, but I was beyond delighted. For days, I was
able to enjoy that beautiful fragrance in my home. Little detail, big
impression.

WHAT STORY DO CUSTOMERS TELL ABOUT YOU?

As important as it is to tell a compelling story about your business,
it's also important to realize that customers are telling their own
versions of your story. If you do a great job crafting your story, they'll
simply repeat it and build upon it. With luck, their embellishments
will be flattering. What do you think people are saying about your
brand? Can your monitoring of social media chatter give you the
inside scoop? Have you conducted any focus groups or surveys to see
how people describe you?

When I think about the brand stories I've developed for the two
companies I've founded (Silver Tree Communications and Silver
Tree Publishing), I hope the client embellishments include mentions
that we never do any overt selling — that we let our insights and
expertise speak for themselves and that we never show up to do

a big "pitch" or a dog-and-pony show for prospective clients. I hope they remember us as thoughtful, focused and kind. In everything we do, we want to be authentic and transparent. A few years ago, a client of mine wrote a recommendation of me on LinkedIn, and I was surprised to see that he said I was funny, which made me fun to work with. I've never thought of humor as my strong suit, and I was delighted. And a few weeks ago, I met a client face-to-face for the first time, and he giggled when I let some swear words tumble out of my mouth. (He admitted he likes "Candid Kate.") I've never thought of my ability to take the work seriously without taking *myself* too seriously as part of my brand story. But according to my clients, it surely is. That's important for me to know.

DON'T JUST HAVE A GREAT STORY – ALSO HAVE A POINT OF VIEW

Today, more than ever, it's important to go beyond the story — to have a personality and to have a unique and meaningful point of view on something (or many things) that matter to your customers. Universities, in particular, are doing a great job of beginning to align themselves with different social views and important issues. Brands used to be afraid to have opinions (about diversity, fairness and public policy), but opinions matter.

Each year, when commercials are unveiled during the "Football-Game-That-Shall-Not-Be-Named-Due-to-Trademark-Laws," we see more brands tying themselves to values and causes — to equality, empowerment, truth, etc. But you don't have to be the kind of company that can afford a television commercial during the aforementioned game to hold a point of view on something important.

Recently, one of our clients, a renowned expert in her field, chose not to publish an article or any social media posts after a major "news day" in her area of expertise. I, for one, was dying to read her take on it all, but she told me "Everyone is writing about it. What more could I possibly add?" I was disappointed. What she didn't seem to appreciate was that her point of view matters, no matter how cluttered the space and how many other people had shared their points of view on the same topic. She has followers and fans, clients and readers, and they wanted to know what *she* was thinking. Still, she didn't think her opinions mattered. She was essentially asking, "Who am I?" "Why would I write this blog post? Nobody's going to read it because EVERYBODY is already talking about this issue." Have you ever said or felt the same way about the opinions and points of view you failed to share?

It is not true that "everybody" is talking about it if *you're* not talking about it. You have constituents who want to hear from you and maybe even new people who would enjoy finding your articles and reading your insights. In refusing to do so, and not taking the time to create blog posts or articles (or op/eds or videos or social media or to stand up and speak at a conference) because "this is a topic that other people have already talked about and done well" you are selling yourself short and depriving the customer. If you have a unique point of view on a point of interest and it is important to the customers you serve, you ought to share it. If you don't share it, people won't know what your views are, and they won't know how to choose you based on whether or not your views, opinions and values align with their own.

Let me ask you this ... In 2016 and 2017, how many articles did you read about the Electoral College? (Did you think "I don't want this expert's opinion. I've already read one or two, and that's plenty." when you reached the second or third article?) And in 2018, how many articles did you read about gun control and mass shootings, about Donald Trump or about immigration policies? (Were you able to stop after just one?)

Each published piece makes us just a little bit sharper. Each article can have value. Remember that your point of view is an extension of your brand story and your company persona, and your followers and stakeholders want to know where you stand. They want to know what *you're* thinking, so go ahead and tell them. Case in point: While entire books have been written about brand storytelling, my book has a chapter about it because I suspect *my* stakeholders want to know *my* take on it. So here you go.

People are afraid to be opinionated today. But brands that are voiceless are invisible.

People are afraid to be opinionated today. But brands that are voiceless are invisible. I'm not suggesting you write bold blog posts about polarizing issues if your business is not tied inextricably to those issues. But your customers and clients should have a sense of your personality. If your customers heard that some sort of scandal happened involving your company name or product, would people clamor to say "Oh, there's no way that happened?" Let me give you an example. I recently heard Southwest Airlines CEO, Gary Kelly, speak about civility and kindness. After hearing him talk about a point of view tied to the company and the way they do business — I would be shocked if their company took actions that were out of sync with that point of view. His willingness to be human and to *have* a point of view elevated the company brand for everyone in the room (though most of us were probably pretty fond of them, to begin with).

Let me share just one more story about brand stories and points of view. There's perhaps nothing more generic than an American fast-casual burger joint, especially in an airport terminal. But last year, I watched my husband wait in line for 20 minutes at a BurgerFi, while I absorbed all the marketing messages. It's fair for me to admit that I have zero interest in burgers — I don't eat meat and I don't eat wheat (i.e., buns). But I was riveted by their story about better-for-you foods, and kindness to animals and the environment. Their beef comes from cattle that are purportedly humanely raised and free-range and that have never been exposed to chemicals or unnecessary drugs. The furniture in their restaurant is upcycled from water bottles and milk cartons. I am convinced, beyond a shadow of a doubt, that the resonance of their story — which hinges on some very strong points of view — is what attracts herds (pardon the pun) of customers to stand in long lines for BurgerFi's premium-priced sandwiches.

STORYTELLING UNDER STRESS: A WORD ABOUT CRISIS COMMUNICATIONS

If you don't know who you are or what you stand for (i.e., if you don't have a clear story), then it becomes exponentially more difficult to find the right messages when you're in a crisis. And if you're in business long enough, you'll likely have a crisis to communicate your way through.

It is my experience that having a great media spokesperson (in-house or on call) can save your brand. They must know your story and your character, long before the crisis strikes, and they must use your brand character to drive the messaging. What do you stand for? What do you believe? If the going gets tough and you stand up in front of television cameras to say that you're heartbroken for the victims, that the error made by your company was an honest mistake or that you're committed to equal pay for equally qualified employees, will your stakeholders believe you? Surviving a media or public relations crisis begins years before, with a clearly articulated and meaningfully different story and believable points of view. Because if you don't have a meaningful story in the minds of your customer *before* the crisis, the crisis will *become* your story.

---

if you don't have a meaningful story in the minds of your customer *before* the crisis, the crisis will *become* your story.

Hopefully, when and if you find yourself dealing with delicate public communications, it won't be because you overtly screwed up. But if that's the case, be sure to check out the "When You Mess Up, Step Up" section in Chapter 12.

Throughout my career, I've handled a great deal of crisis response and post-crisis storytelling for clients and employers. I've handled everything from:

- Protecting medical facilities from looking heartless when they must close down a research trial that appeared to be helping breast cancer patients, to

- Setting the record straight during sexual harassment scandals, to

- Calming protestors seeking an audience with an elected official, to

- Clarifying the complex details of a class-action pollution lawsuit in the rural Midwest.

In every one of those cases, my success hinged on whether I was "thinking like a marketer." Because you see, a marketer would think *how will our public statement on this matter ultimately impact sales and customer sentiment? How will this align with our brand personality? What do the community and the media need and deserve from us right now, even if it's painful or humbling for us to give?* Thinking that way can keep your company alive.

Unfortunately, crisis communications decisions are often made by leaders who aren't marketing-minded — but who are instead emotional and single-minded people trying to answer the complaint, defend their company's honor, or come off as right or tough or having the last word. But being *right* and being *tough* isn't always what is in your best interests in the long term. Crisis communication is about controlling the narrative, and sometimes telling a completely new or expanded story building upon what people already know about you, and shifting sentiment and reiterating what you stand for, who you are and why you matter to the marketplace or to the community. Storytelling under stress is the most difficult and important storytelling of all.

Storytelling under stress is the most difficult and important storytelling of all.

THE FUTURE OF BRAND STORYTELLING

Perhaps one of the most valuable things I can do in this book is to provide some informed predictions of what's on the horizon. Knowing what's happening now and how to excel in the moment is vital, but the health of your company and your career depends upon your ability to apply your fresh marketing mindset in new ways as the

??? *ASK YOURSELF ...*

A vital part of telling your brand story is telling the story of your customers. Because without their story, your story wouldn't matter.

ASK Yourself ...

If you had to shoot a video this week focusing simply on who chooses your company's services or products, could you do it in a compelling way? Do you know how your customers fit into perhaps a few different sub-segments, and what makes them different? Do you understand what they care about, what problems they are seeking to solve, what aspirations they have, what fears they harbor, or how much money they are willing to spend with you? Do you know your customer? Challenge yourself to talk about them — in depth and with the kind of empathy that creates connection.

world of business evolves around you. I encourage you to take the time to linger over these final snippets of each chapter, where I'll offer predictions, tips and strategic advice about how to stay ahead of the curve. As Walter Gretzky once told his son Wayne about the game of hockey "Skate to where the puck is going, not to where it has been."

My predictions? Customers will increasingly make you "prove it" when you tell a story and make a brand promise. Savvy consumers (like Gen Z, who are fearless about calling out bullshit) are sick of generic messages. If you're a community college with the tagline

"Start here, go anywhere," consumers will consider you generic —
because any community college could use that tagline. Challenge
yourself and your company to be "the product or service *that ... "*
[fill in the blank]. "The consultant or doctor or attorney *who ... "*
[again, fill in the blank]. Make that sentence — that "brand promise"
to your customer — as specific and meaningful as possible. *Be
meaningfully different.* I also predict that brand stories will get
shorter and more poignant, and they will be told with more images,
sound, motion and fewer words. They will be told in the voice of the
customer, not the voice of the brand. And more industry-leading,
couldn't-catch-them-if-you-tried companies (like Southwest
Airlines) will empower every single employee to share, tell and
evolve the story.

GETTING BACK TO THE PRINCIPLES

Storytelling and the Think Like a Marketer *Principles*

A powerful, meaningfully different story is vital to your business and
should underpin everything you do. The core story should influence
how you talk about your people, your products, your services, your
customers and even fleeting messages, like next week's sidewalk sale
or your speaking engagement at the executive's club. But two principles, in particular, should guide your commitment to your story.

Principle #1: Communicate for connection and meaning, not just to transact sales

The story of your business, of your expertise and of your product or
service offerings should always be analyzed from the perspective of
the customer or client. Be sure your story resonates with the people

you're trying to reach and take the time to tell your story continuously, not just when you're worried about 3rd-quarter earnings or stressed out about whether you have enough RSVPs for your public webinar tomorrow.

Principle #4: Create cultures and processes that align with your brand

If your brand is about quality, comfort and social responsibility, and you've been telling a brand story that paints you out to be the kindest shoe company the average consumer has ever "met," be sure your cultures and processes are guided by the story. Ensure your employee culture lives up to the story's promise and hype, and that your processes (like "when the customer buys a pair of shoes, we donate a pair to someone in need") align with the brand.

. . . .

03

GIVE IT AWAY!

(Because They Can't Know if They Love You if They've Never Sampled Your Product)

When it comes to great marketing strategies, some things never change. Sure — the media options are vast and powerful now, and people are broadcasting live videos from their mobile phones. And yes, consumers are more demanding and fickle than ever. But basic human psychology hasn't changed. People want to buy products and services they can trust, and no one wants to commit to anything that's new and unproven.

Enter the "sampling strategy." If you have ever eaten a free Bagel Bite on a tiny napkin in the aisle of a grocery store, you have "sampled" a product. And if you then *bought* a box of Bagel Bites, you have made the marketers very happy. Today, sampling is alive and well but is taking on new and innovative forms.

SAMPLING STRATEGIES FOR EVERY INDUSTRY

"But I'm a B2B marketer," you might say. Or "My product or service isn't something that can be sampled." Think again.

Here are just a few examples to spur your thinking about how you can turn customer awareness into EXPERIENCE and interest, and thus into preference and purchase intent.

You can turn customer awareness into EXPERIENCE and interest, and thus into preference and purchase intent.

Higher Education

The savvy undergraduate universities offer activity-packed "prospective student weekends" where future coeds can get the chance to "live" the genuine college experience. And don't forget to take those kids to the bookstore to buy a sweatshirt with the university logo on it. But can "sampling" work for professional schools like medical schools, business schools or law schools? Absolutely. I've had the honor of working on developing wonderful, industry-best sampling opportunities for Rosalind Franklin University of Medicine and Science and Lake Forest Graduate School of Management. Rosalind Franklin has offered a community Mini Medical School (no cost!) for four weeks so prospective students, area business professionals and retirees can learn about DNA, diabetes, Alzheimer's, cadaver labs and more. This University also has championed a collaboration with LeadAmerica to host a summer conference for high school students who are interested in healthcare careers. These types of sampling experiences provide goodwill to the community, and ultimately convert into student tuition revenue, philanthropic support and new patients for the University's health system. As for Lake Forest Graduate School, their marketing and admissions process hinges on an unrivaled open house experience they call the MBA Preview, where busy professionals spend just two hours at a campus and get to meet students, faculty, and alumni, and participate in an actual in-session MBA class. When I last had access to their conversion metrics, nearly 50% of prospective students who'd attended an MBA Preview enrolled.

Retail Products

We've established that if you sell food, you can always give away a little taste (at grocery stores, at your restaurant/café, or at community food fairs). But what if you sell expensive, high-involvement products, like specialty outdoor gear? Do what Northerly Outfitters did to help tentative winter sports enthusiasts try out new activities — offer snowshoe rentals! Talk about a great, low-commitment way to see what the experience is all about. In recent years, many retail companies have offered subscription boxes or have gotten their products inserted into boxes being marketed, sold and distributed by others. (Have you ever ordered some batteries or a hoodie, and found a sample-sized package of laundry detergent in the box?) Get creative and you'll discover you can provide samples of your product this way too, whether you sell dog toys, organic snacks for humans, or cosmetics.

Home Improvement

The Lowes Build and Grow program for kids is a clever way to teach your children new skills, as it allows Lowes to get you into the building spirit. I have no doubt parents who bring their kids in for the workshops end up buying products during their visit. And another, more obvious and direct sampling concept (in that the sampling experience is had by the actual consumer and not their children or grandchildren) is the series of workshops offered at Home Depot, in which do-it-yourselfers can learn how to hang window treatments, install a closet organizer or toilet, or plant flower beds the neighbors will envy.

Professional Services

Even consultants can get into the sampling game. My friend Doug LaBelle at LaBelle Training offered, at his former company, no-cost "sample" seminars on topics like diversity and service excellence, to would-be corporate clients. Because hospitals and other large prospective clients are apt to hesitate over flying in a facilitator, paying thousands of dollars and taking 30 people off the floor for the day, providing a training course to those prospective clients at no fee (they simply pick up the travel expenses) was a bold and innovative solution for Doug and his former business partner. In fact, they turned 50% of all "pilot program" clients into real, paying clients. He also asks those benefitting from a free course, "Because we're doing this pilot for free, would it be okay if I invited one person from another area company to attend?" Inevitably, the answer is yes.

A great many paid professional speakers offer "samples" by facilitating free lunch-and-learn programs at area corporations, and pre-contract, no-cost consultations also make a valuable offering, whether you're a financial planner, marketing consultant, physician or attorney.

With the ease and affordability of online publishing (on social channels as well as your own website), it's possible for brands in all industries and of all sizes to use content marketing as part (or all) of their sampling strategy. How can blogging, social media and even custom tips and advice that you give away for free attract value to the bottom line? Sampling is all about the create value/capture value cycle. Create value for the customer through the sample product or experience and capture value for the business in the end.

Create value for the customer through the sample product or experience and capture value for the business in the end.

Even if you sell a physical product, you don't have to be face-to-face with the customer to provide a sample. For example, the folks at Canyon Bakehouse (who make non-GMO, zero-gluten breads and other products) have made it utterly simple for customers to get free products (through coupons) by engaging with them on social media and on their website. I, for one, plan to sample their products soon and already feel endeared to them for letting me try out their premium selections at no cost and no risk.

And not all samples need to be free. They just need to be "bite-sized," low cost, convenient and commitment-free. I may be a little biased (as I own a book publishing company), but I think of the business book as the ultimate sampling strategy for consultants, coaches, speakers and other thought leaders. How do I know what I'm buying if I hire strategic thinking expert Rich Horwath to lead a strategic planning engagement? I read one of his books (like his bestsellers *Deep Dive* and *Elevate*) to find out. How do I know that female consumerism expert Bridget Brennan will deliver in massive ways if I hire her for a keynote? Because her first book, *Why She Buys*, taught me so much. How can I be sure that Cara Silletto could help my organization keep its employees longer? Because the breakthrough ideas I'm already implementing were inspired by the insights in her book, *Staying Power*. See Chapter 7 of *this* book for more about writing and marketing a nonfiction book as part of your own *Think Like a Marketer* strategy. And yes, this book is *my* sample. I suspect and hope that clients interested in hiring me for brand storytelling services will flip immediately to Chapter 2, and those considering hiring me for market research might find it incredibly helpful to hear my take on customer insights in Chapter 13 before calling me to schedule an initial consultation. What better way to "test drive" the quality of my thinking or the value of my ideas and processes than to spend a few hours, at very low cost, hearing me talk about the prin-ciples I use when helping great brands — big and small, global and domestic — take their marketing to the next level?

Whether a "sample" in your industry is a bite of cheesecake, a free webinar, or a ride around the block on a scooter, I encourage you to think about how to create these customer experiences as part of your marketing and sales cycle. While not every product or service that you are tasked with marketing might lend itself *easily* to a sampling strategy, I'm convinced there's always a way to give the customer what they need — an enjoyable experience that's low commitment and leaves them wanting more.

THE FUTURE OF SAMPLING

Savvy business leaders and marketers will constantly reinvent the concept of sampling. I predict innovative new couponing ideas and the leveraging of social connection (one sample for you, one for you to share with a friend). Be on the lookout for BOGO offers at places other than shoe stores (like business authors who give you a free copy of the book if you buy one, so you can pass the second copy along to a colleague or friend — so you're more likely to feel the kind of gratitude that motivates a 5-star review on Amazon). Different from, but related to, sampling is selling on consignment, so to speak — as is the case with consultants who don't charge for their services if the client doesn't get results, or who take their profits on the back end through a commission or royalty. Early in this book, I mentioned the Caterpillar dirt playground; it is my hope that big brands selling big-ticket items will continue to offer *big surprises* like this when it comes to offering "samples" to the marketplace.

ASK YOURSELF ...

Not everything has an obvious sample strategy, and it's my guess that 99% of the readers of this book don't sell Bagel Bites. So, you sometimes have to get creative.

ASK yourself ...

If budget and logistics were no issue, what creative sampling strategy would you roll out next quarter for your top product or service (or the new one you're trying to get to "take off")?

By the way, I wrote the first draft of this chapter from my Microsoft Surface at an Argo Tea Café in downtown Chicago, where, when I arrived, an employee was handing out tiny cups of Carolina Honey iced tea to passersby on the busy street corner. Mmmm ... samples. Case in point.

· ·

GETTING BACK TO THE PRINCIPLES

Sampling and the Think Like a Marketer *Principles*

Think back to the 5 principles of "thinking like a marketer." Providing samples to your customers allows you to serve several of the key principles.

Principle #1: Communicate for connection and meaning, not just to transact sales

If your samples are a kind of content marketing (like blog posts or podcasts), they are also communications efforts. And if you're doing it right, they don't always end with a "go here" or "buy now" call to action. They transcend the urge to transact short-term sales.

Principle #3: Market in a way that's strategy-religious and tactic-agnostic

Many of you have probably never thought about a sampling opportunity for your products or services. But sampling initiatives are tactics that might serve a larger strategy to which you are committed. Don't be afraid to try something new.

**Principle #4: Create cultures and processes that align
with your brand**

If your brand is all about generosity or hospitality or experience or
fun, giving away "free samples" might be a perfect fit for your brand.

**Principle #5: Do everything in service of maintaining a virtuous
cycle of creating value for the customer while capturing
value for you**

Samples are all about "bits of value" for customers. When done well,
the capture of value will naturally follow.

04

DON'T GIVE IT ALL AWAY, FOR HEAVEN'S SAKE!

(Monetize It!)

Okay, so I've just made a hard sell in the previous chapter on giving away your products, services or insights as a way to build your brand and attract a customer base. And I meant every word. But I'm including this follow-up chapter because some good-hearted business owners and leaders don't know how to stop themselves from giving it ALL away. If you remember our Create Value/Capture Value model, you'll have to admit that it's imperative to get to the "capturing value" part at some point.

Keep blogging and offering samples, but also keep your sampling and content marketing in balance with business development and actual productive work you can invoice for.

Keep blogging and offering samples, but also keep your sampling and content marketing in balance with business development and actual productive work you can invoice for. While it should be obvious to business owners and business leaders that the whole point of being in business is to do so profitably, I have worked with more clients than I can count who didn't know how to price their products and services or who were exhausting themselves producing a podcast that had no demonstrable value on their balance sheet — no paid advertising, no fees associated with appearing on the show, and no measurable evidence that podcast listeners were becoming customers or that they were willing to pay higher prices based on the value of the podcast.

It's my experience that some people — typically solopreneurs and consultants who specialize in soft skills — think that getting paid is a perk they don't deserve or that it is at odds with their compassionate demeanor. I mentioned in the introduction that this book was inspired, in part, by a client who is sharp and works like the dickens, but who isn't selling advertising on his forums and content. He's not thinking like a marketer. One of the questions I am constantly asking when I see new businesses and brands crop up is, "How do they monetize it?" Or "When will they monetize it?" If you're a well-funded start-up looking to prove a concept and attract a following, sometimes you need to subsist off investment funding until you're able to monetize your concept. Certainly, Facebook took years before introducing paid services (like advertising), and even Amazon operated at a loss until it became so ubiquitous that it could negotiate better margins with its vendors and shipping partners and until it could sell the world on its Prime membership.

In our book publishing business, we work with two kinds of authors: those who make money from their books and those who don't. The authors who have no strategy for making back the investment typically don't. They fail to increase their speaking fees or negotiate with corporate clients regarding the inclusion of bulk book orders as part of their contracts. But other authors kill it when it comes to the monetization of their books — they produce custom B2B editions for corporate clients (with client branding and even a foreword from the client's CEO) and are selling hundreds or even thousands of books each month as a value-add to the other services they offer (like speaking, training and consulting). They see their book as part of their brand offering, and they're not afraid to ask to be paid. What has value for the customer can and should eventually generate value for the business.

SOME PRACTICAL TIPS ON KEEPING THE CASH FLOWING IN

- *Adjust your product prices or service fees over time.* If your costs to produce your goods are going up, if the value of your products or services is increasing to the customer, and/or if you're continually adding value to what you provide to the marketplace, you need to think about what you charge and how to make appropriate adjustments over time. Often, those adjustments will be price increases. But sometimes a price *decrease* can attract a higher volume of sales and can put more money in the bank, so don't automatically deduce that "charging more" will be the way to go. If you're not sure how your prices and fees stack up against the competition or what your customers are willing to pay, do the research to find out.

- *Put your best talent and resources toward the activities, services and products that generate the most efficient profits to yield high margins.* Learn how to say "no" to low-margin opportunities or distracting marketing tactics. Resist the urge to "grow" the business by adding to your product or service line if doing so is to the detriment of the bottom line and increases the exhaustion of your people. Focus is key. Can you focus on fewer offerings and do away with the ones that don't generate money efficiently? Let me share a common mistake that not-for-profit marketers make because it's an example that saddens me and one that is relevant to all readers of this book. Lots of charities hold signature fundraising events — gala nights, golf outings, champagne brunches, 5K walk/runs, etc. And most charities can convince themselves that exhausting their entire staff (and an army of volunteers) for six months with the time it takes to plan and execute an event that generates $75,000 is something they can't stop doing (because they can't "lose" that $75,000). But the truth of the matter is that most organizations would generate more profit more efficiently if they got out of the party-planning business and put their energies into grant writing and corporate relationship stewardship. Events are vital for brand education, donor stewardship and attraction of new stakeholders, but often one well-executed, truly engaging event per year will do. Monetization of your organization is not just about making money — it's about making *enough* money from the right sources in an efficient and repeatable manner.

Monetization of your organization is not just about making money — it's about making *enough* money from the right sources in an efficient and repeatable manner.

- *Have processes in place to prevent scope creep if your business provides professional services.* As of the writing of this book, my company has been in business for 16 years. Our contracts in our first several years weren't particularly sophisticated and left us open to too many opportunities for disaster — due to clients who wanted extra services or a dozen rounds of changes to their project. These derailments left me exhausted and sometimes caused me to lose money instead of making it. It wasn't until a few years ago that I began using formal "Change Orders" to amend and expand contracts for clients whose needs and expectations evolved over time. In the end, you must value yourself (and your team, your brand and your other assets) so you don't burn out, and so you don't hurt your reputation (e.g., by being perceived as low-cost or unprofessional) and also ... so you don't go broke.

- *Want to "give it away" but can't afford to? Get someone else to pay for it.* We live in changing times when it comes to retail, and the rise in popularity of "subscription boxes" is a notable example. Think about how to insert a sample of your product into a subscription box or the shipping boxes of another popular company's products. Consider selling advertising on your blog or podcast site, so someone other than the end user can pick up the tab. And don't forget to think about underwriting and sponsorship opportunities — you can secure paid sponsors for everything from a book launch party to a commercial you're running on YouTube.

- *Have a bigger, better, monetized version of the content and samples you give away for free.* In the consumer retail space, selling baskets and boxes of product samples can open up new sources of revenue. In the consulting and professional services arenas, you should be thinking about how to reassemble existing content to make it so valuable that you can put a price tag on it. If you're a blogger or writer, pick up a copy of Cathy Fyock's *Blog2Book: Repurposing Content to Discover the Book You've Already Written*; turning your articles and blogs into a book is a great way to create new value for customers and capture more value for you. If your organization (whether it's an insurance company, a leadership consulting firm, a medical practice or a law firm) has insights aplenty on hot topics in your industry, consider creating a report or white paper you can use for high-end, high-value business development or as an offer made through email or on the web in exchange for signing up for your mailing list. At Silver Tree, we have conducted market research with thousands of college-bound high school students and their parents and have done so on behalf of many universities. The non-proprietary insights from that collective research are being evolved into key portions of a white paper for the higher education industry. Always be thinking about derivative works or evolved products and services that build upon what you're already doing. There is no shortage of ways to create more value and capture more value if you'll *think like a marketer* to discover them.

Always be thinking about derivative works or evolved products and services that build upon what you're already doing. There is no shortage of ways to create more value and capture more value if you'll *think like a marketer* to discover them.

THE "BUSINESS PITCH" DILEMMA

Have you ever been asked to give away your best thinking (your proverbial secret sauce) as a way to earn new business or win over a client? Did it make you uncomfortable or resentful? This is a serious dilemma faced by agencies and consultants who are asked to present how they would solve a business problem as part of their new business pitch. This practice is happening for the deep-pocket consulting firms and for individual coaches and consultants alike. I happen to think it's outright robbery. As such, it's my own practice not to

?!? ASK YOURSELF ...

You and your products and services are valuable. So, while it's vital that you tell a story establishing that value, never capturing benefit or bringing value back to the bottom line is a failure. Companies that succeed through sustainable processes are thoughtful and strategic about the balance between what they give away and what they sell.

ASK yourself ...

What are you currently giving away that someone (customer, sponsor, advertiser, partner) would be more than willing to pay for? Is giving away too much value actually making you less credible and driving your other prices down? Do you have any idea what the price sensitivity is for your key money makers (i.e., what customers or clients would really be willing to pay for the products and services that are core to your business)?

respond to ridiculous requests for proposals (RFPs) or do any significant preparatory work for no-cost consultations with prospective clients. I am more than happy to spend an hour sharing my thoughts and approaches with a future customer to let them "sample" my thinking and understand the value of what they'd be buying if they hire me, but I try hard not to dedicate hours to pre-work that is true consulting or creative development disguised as unpaid business development. (By way of example, our graphic designers aren't going to sketch out a book cover concept during a live video call with you and let you take a photograph or screen grab of their sketch if you're still a prospective client. Creative ideation work and initial concepting for illustrations is work for which we should be paid.) Sure, I periodically rattle off an idea during a pitch meeting that a would-be client turns into a billboard headline or a strategic initiative for which I never receive compensation. And I'm okay with that. It's my experience that giving a prospective customer a little "ah-ha" for free can get them to hire you for the big "ah-has" later. But the big "ah-has" come with a price tag. If your business is suffering through the challenge of solving other people's problems for free during complex pitch meetings, I strongly urge you to say "no" or to change your approach. It's the client's job to either solve their problems themselves or to *hire* you to solve them together. Tricking you into solving them for free under the pretense that maybe you'll land a big contract is disrespectful. Why would you want to work for a client who refused to value you from "hello?"

THE FUTURE OF SMART MONETIZATION

Smart business leaders know when to monetize (and when to give products and services away). In the future, they'll be even more strategic and subtle about how and when to charge, so customers never feel "up-sold" or "nickeled and dimed" to death. They'll be more creative in understanding that the customer who consumes their products or services doesn't always have to be the one paying for it. I predict that "qualified subscription" models will come back in force (like the financial model that drives trade magazines, where qualified professionals get subscriptions for free, and the advertisers foot the bill), that affiliate marketing will continue to evolve in powerful ways, and that companies will discover creative methods to offer tiered and customized products and services with a full range of price points.

GETTING BACK TO THE PRINCIPLES

Monetization and the Think Like a Marketer *Principles*

All five of the *Think Like a Market*er principles, when applied effectively, will positively impact your bottom line. But the moral of this chapter's story is about balancing the give and take of value, and so one principle, in particular, is most relevant.

Principle #5: Do everything in service of maintaining a virtuous cycle of creating value for the customer while capturing value for you

It's nice to be nice. It's generous to be generous. But you're in business to stay in business, so you must never lose sight of how to make the cash register ring.

05

LOVE (AND PROTECT!) YOUR DATABASE OR LOSE YOUR COMPANY

When it comes to running a successful company, many activities qualify as fun, exciting and interesting. But, for most of us, taking care of the database is not one of them. Mind-numbing as it may be to organize, clean and cull your prospect and customer lists on a regular basis, refusing to do this work and do it well can be the death-knell for otherwise promising companies. Ultimately, marketing comes down to two simple steps: 1) Finding your customers, and 2) communicating the right messages with them (in the right ways, at the right time). Of course, finding (and keeping) them is all about your database.

Mind-numbing as it may be to organize, clean and cull your prospect and customer lists on a regular basis, refusing to do this work and do it well can be the death-knell for otherwise promising companies.

Whether you're worried about existing customers, warm leads or strangers ripe for the prospecting, ask yourself: *If I can't reach them at all right now, how do I expect to reach into their wallets tomorrow?*

START WITH A HIGH-QUALITY LIST

When it comes to direct-response marketing (e.g., marketing where you're reaching out to touch customers one at a time by putting an email in their inbox or a postcard in their mailbox), I'm convinced that most projects fall apart not because the postcard wasn't pretty or the call-to-action wasn't compelling, but that that the list failed. Renting or purchasing direct mail (DM) lists isn't sexy (and third-party email lists, thanks to the CAN-SPAM Act, are almost impossible to procure), building a great list is Herculean work, and running a report from your own database can be a disaster if it's full of holes. Notably, marketers tend to rush to the creative — writing witty headlines and choosing evocative stock photos to convey their message. But the list — and whether it leads you to the right customers, and enough of them — will make or break you.

I once heard a marketer at a print production company assert that 40% of the success of a direct mail program is dependent on the list, and I'd wager that the dependence might be even higher. (For my detailed thoughts on direct mail as a marketing tactic, be sure to read Chapter 6, where I say more on this topic, and read the bonus chapter on direct mail at SilverTreeCommunications.com/DM) Even when you have a good partner for purchasing or compiling lists, it's easy to make mistakes. In my career, I've seen MBA programs mail expensive packages to six-year-olds, and I've acquired lists from B2B data experts like Hoovers that were more than 25% undeliverable. If you don't already have a lot of customers or prospects who have provided their contact information, don't assume you can simply purchase a list of names to save the day. It's increasingly difficult to find a list vendor you can trust to deliver, and their prices can be astronomical.

When it comes to B2B lists, I have found the highest quality data comes from your own customer relationship management (CRM) system or from membership associations that rent lists. The best sales prospects for an industrial products' company's newest offerings, for example, are typically their current and previous customers. But if you're a medical malpractice insurance company looking to attract attendees to a patient safety conference, it's smart to consider targeting the current members of the American Society of Healthcare Risk Managers (through the various methods the Society makes available to advertisers, like newsletters and dedicated email promotions). But starting with a great list doesn't keep you golden for long. Even your own high-quality, carefully managed list goes stale quickly; 18-20% of the population moves every year, and 10-15% of businesses move or stop operating annually. Cell phone numbers often stay the same as people move, but home and business addresses and even business email addresses constantly become obsolete. When it comes to keeping your list current, you can't blink, or you'll lose your customers.

A current and accurate list can still be a *worthless* list.

Let me also add that a current and accurate list can still be a *worthless* list. When I first joined the graduate business school where I served as a marketing director, our prospective MBA student database was full of names of people who didn't really seem interested in talking to our admissions managers. It turned out that the list contained, in addition to all the people who were actively interested in applying for admission, names of people who had dropped their business cards in fish bowls at community events. These people had little to no interest in getting an MBA, but they just wanted to be entered into a drawing to win a cool prize. So while a robust mailing list is vital, you're only hurting yourself if you start kidding yourself about the value of your leads. Someone who has come right out and said they are interested in paying for your products or services is a very different kind of prospect than someone who gave you their card during a raffle or who provided an email so they could download a white paper on a hot topic.

PROTECT YOUR LIST: IT'S ABOUT LOVE AND RESPECT

It should go without saying that spamming your customer list is unkind and bad business, but it's still too common a practice — even by otherwise solid brands and well-meaning professionals — for me not to address. In my mind, "spamming" is repeated, needy, pushy, unnecessary communication of any kind — calling too often, sending too many emails, and putting too much "junk mail" in the mailboxes of the people you purport to value.

Over-communicating is a type of bad customer service that you can't afford to deliver. It's too easy for people to hit an email "unsub-scribe" button, and not much more difficult for them to call and request that you never mail or call them again. Even when they don't officially opt out of your list, a huge portion of people who are feeling "spammed" simply stop listening. Your postcards go in the trash without a glance, your emails get deleted and your calls go to voicemail. Do you have any idea what that's costing you? New customer acquisition costs vary widely by industry, but it's always cheaper to keep your customers and followers than it is to acquire new ones. Some estimates indicate the cost of finding and engaging a new customer is 5 to 25 times the cost of retaining one.

If you are realizing your database is valuable and vital now, just think about what it can be worth in the future. Remember that when you sell a company, one of the most valuable assets, perhaps aside from patents and real estate, is the customer and prospect list. Nobody wants to own or run your business if there aren't customers aplenty lined up at the (literal or virtual) door. Your customer and prospect lists can determine whether you can retire sooner rather than later if you're an entrepreneur, and whether anyone wants to fill your shoes, work for you or invest in your company if you're a corporate leader. Your database is a priceless asset, and you must treat it that way NOW.

Remember that when you sell a company, one of the most valuable assets, perhaps aside from patents and real estate, is the customer and prospect list.

MORE THAN A LIST ... A FULL PIPELINE

Thriving companies know that success is all about a full pipeline. What do I mean by a "pipeline?" A pipeline is a ready-made flow of prospective customers who are always learning about your brand and showing up at your front door, wallets open and ready to engage — even though you might not know their names (i.e., they might not be in your database yet).

Examples of vital pipeline relationships that help companies thrive include:

- Graduate degree programs that are part of the same college or university or affiliated formally with similar undergraduate programs. (E.g., If Susan earns her bachelor's degree in biology, with a pre-med focus, at a university that has a medical school, that medical school can feel fairly confident that Susan will apply for admission to their MD program.) *If you've ever heard of a higher education institution offering a "3+2" or similar "combined degree" program, where a student rolls straight from their undergraduate studies into their graduate studies without having to apply to the graduate school, you've seen a pipeline strategy in action.*

- Media outlets (like magazines and cable networks) that deliver national and international news and have received thousands or even millions of readers/clicks because social networks like Facebook push their articles into the data feeds of users, even when the media outlet doesn't pay for advertising. *It's important to respect the fact that this type of pipeline can dry up. In 2018, Facebook prioritized content in its users' News Feeds so that media outlets got lower priority than content from a user's friends, family and groups; as a result, traffic to Slate.com (which previously received the majority of its readership via its Facebook pipeline) saw its website traffic decline by 87%.*

- Professional services organizations that have delighted some clients who are affiliated with a professional association, where people enthusiastically provide recommendations. (E.g., The publishing business that I own has represented several authors who are prominent and well-respected members of the National Speakers Association. As such, we can typically count on a healthy number of leads from NSA-affiliated authors each year.) *Where is your company a rock star? If you have a few top sources of business or referrals, be sure to treat your relationship with those organizations with care and commitment.*

- Sister businesses or divisions that engage customers for one purpose and then increase the likelihood that they'll stay brand-loyal for another purchase. (E.g., If David sells his car to CarMax, he becomes part of a pipeline of consumers who might then buy a car from CarMax.) *Does your company have a lower-commitment point of entry that could warm up a pipeline for further business? Think about how you've gotten comfortable with a brand before committing in big ways — by renting a condo before buying it or attending a webinar or workshop before hiring a consultant for a larger engagement.*

- Non-competing businesses that know people who need your products or services. (E.g., Kim gets regular skin health services from her dermatologist, who refers her to a plastic surgeon for a tummy tuck after the fillers in her face give her more confidence about her body.) *What brands are selling products and services to your ideal customers right now? Can you make yourself known to key leaders at those businesses to potentially put your company's offerings on the tip of the tongue and top of the mind for those referrers?*

If you've ever had a water-main break in your neighborhood and gone without water for a day or more, you know that pipelines are imperative. Similarly, in your business, it's crucial that you understand what feeds your pipeline and that you take good care of it.

LIST OR PIPELINE, BIGGER IS BETTER BUT QUALITY BEATS SIZE

Think about companies that are growing rapidly and that truly impress you. Unless they provide a unique, can't-live-without product that no one else sells, chances are that their meteoric rise is related, at least in part, to a very smart list building and/or pipeline creation strategy. They keep building the list, and they keep it clean. If someone on their email list doesn't open messages for six months, they remove them from the list. If someone on their direct mail list hasn't placed an order or gotten in touch for more than a year, they stop mailing catalogs to them. If they've called and left 12 voice messages this fiscal quarter for a young woman who has not engaged with their brand in any way they can measure, they stop calling her. Some of the companies and brands that I think are doing the best job in this regard (without ever making customers feel "lured" or sold to) are Chris Brogan (social media expert, bestselling author and CEO of Owner Media Group), Marie Forleo (life coach, author and award-winning host of MarieTV), and Canyon Bakehouse (a gluten-free bakery that has a touching story and a generous approach to sampling, couponing and content sharing).

Size matters. We can pay a hefty price when we maintain small databases — just think about the man-hours spent on developing a promotion (investments in photography, graphic design, copy-writing and more) that only serves a small group of people. Set-up costs can be significant for marketing tactics and, therefore, it often costs you almost as much to communicate to 500 people as it does to reach 5,000 people, but your results, of course, will vary drastically. The more people at the top of the proverbial funnel (i.e., in your initial list or pipeline, before people start to ignore you, opt out or engage/buy), the more customers you'll have left in the end. Imagine that you work in an industry that has relatively stable "open rates" for its mass emails (i.e., the percentage of people opening your emails is pretty predictable over time). If 16% of your list opens your emails and 2% of them convert into sales, you can project your financials each month based on the size of your list. And, well, 2% of a little list won't pay as many bills as 2% of a huge list. Growth is everything.

In some circles, the size of the universe you can reach is called a "platform." Celebrities and authors are among those who are concerned with building a large platform and amassing a large audience. And just as is the case with sales pipelines and customer lists/databases, bigger platforms hold the most promise. One of my clients was recently on a nationally syndicated television show with more than four million viewers per episode; as a result of that appearance, her book sold 200 copies on Amazon. With a sales conversion of just a tiny fraction of a percentage point, that client still grew her own brand and made some money in the process. Four million people is an enviable "top of the funnel" platform. Platform sizes matter to book publishers too, and a platform includes followers and fans on Facebook, LinkedIn, Twitter, Instagram and SnapChat. A marketing client recently confided that she almost lost a book deal with Harper Collins (who was chasing *her*, by the way!) because they worried she didn't have a large enough platform to ultimately translate into enough book sales.

When it comes to pipelines and databases, it's about knowing enough people to turn awareness into interest and interest into purchase.

When it comes to pipelines and databases, it's about knowing enough people to turn awareness into interest and interest into purchase. The numbers matter. Go big or go home when it comes to your followers (on your list and on social media). But those numbers only matter if they represent the right kind of people. (Remember the story about the business cards in the fish bowls.) It doesn't make sense to mail your expensive catalog to someone who has only made one small purchase with you in the past five years, or to keep sending articles and offers to a prospective consulting client who likes to "pick your brain" (i.e., sucker you into some free consulting) but who has never signed a contract for a paid engagement. A medium-sized, high-quality list is more valuable any day of the week than a huge

?? ASK YOURSELF ...

Knowing that size and quality matter when it comes to maintaining a list that drives money to your bottom line, there's surely more you can do in this regard.

ASK yourself ...

What can you do in the next 90 days to reduce your email opt-out (unsubscribe) rate? How can you lower your chances of losing the people you worked so hard to find?

list full of bad information or people who aren't likely to convert into paying customers.

Why do stores like Target and Walgreens spend so much time and money on rewards programs? They want to know who you are ... because *knowing* you and knowing how to reach you are the gateway to increased revenue — increased share of wallet, more return visits, etc. The more they know about you, the more effectively they can determine whether you're a high-quality contact, worthy of printed mailings and special offers.

Remember the chapter on sampling? Think about how you can connect a sampling strategy to your list-building strategy. What can you give away in exchange for contact information? A simple "sign up for our list" is not all that enticing, but companies that throw in a special offer can successfully collect more contact information. Customers who opt into a mailing list want to know what's in it for them! When I readily handed off my information to Canyon Bakehouse, I did it for a coupon I could use the very next day at a local grocer.

THE FUTURE OF LIST DEVELOPMENT AND NURTURING

As businesses get savvier about getting you on their list, you won't even realize you've joined a list! I predict that smart companies will engage in deep segmentation — letting you receive correspondence about sales and coupons while allowing you to opt out of event invitations or giving you six different ways to have your newsletter organized and delivered to you — so no one unsubscribes "all the way." I also look forward to innovative new ways to keep lists (like social followers, text/phone lists, etc.) and new ways to make customers comfortable with these evolutions.

It's about having their ear, their heart and their loyalty so that even when you can't find them, they are always purposefully *finding you*.

Maintaining a sales and marketing database used to be about having the prospect or customer's mailing address, then their phone, then their email. Now? It's more about having their ear, their heart and their loyalty so that even when you can't find them, they are always purposefully *finding you*.

. . . .

GETTING BACK TO THE PRINCIPLES

List Management and the Think Like a Marketer *Principles*

The right list and the right pipeline can set a company on fire and positively impact nearly every strategy and initiative you have in place. This work is most tightly tied to these two *Think Like a Marketer* principles ...

Principle #1: Communicate for connection and meaning, not just to transact sales

If all you ever say to the people on your mailing list is "buy now," they'll eventually say, "bye now." Don't spam your list and don't be greedy about why you're reaching out in the first place.

Principle #4: Create cultures and processes that align with your brand

How you build, maintain and clean your list, as well as how you use the valuable and sacred information on that list, shouldn't be by accident. Think of your database or your pipeline as people attending a very expensive cocktail party you're hosting. Treat them well, and in alignment with your brand and your story.

. . . .

06

DON'T PURSUE ALL THE MARKETING TACTICS

(Many Are a Waste of Your Time!), But Always Be Open to New Ones

For marketers and non-marketers alike, knowing what marketing tactics to pursue and which to dismiss can be a daily struggle, especially when others are second-guessing us with "You should do more video!" and "Does your company have an app?" I am a strong believer in being open-minded, nimble and unapologetic about testing different marketing tactics — if something appears to fit your strategy and your brand personality, and you can afford to test it out, then try it. But if it's not working (or you're unable to measure whether it's working or not), be willing to reallocate resources to try something new.

I believe so strongly in being what I call *strategy-religious and tactic-agnostic* that it's *Think Like a Marketer* Principle #3! Be relentlessly focused on your business strategy and your marketing strategy (i.e., be "religious" about it), but be willing to apply whichever tactics best serve your customers (i.e., be "agnostic" about your loyalties to radio commercials vs. email marketing), even if those tactics are hard to execute or not as fun and sexy as the latest-and-greatest digital channel. Be willing to produce videos and webinars even if that scares you. Be willing to take on the challenge of public speaking, even if you're not good at it yet. Be willing to try your hand at public relations (like pitching a story to a trade journal or making an appearance on a local television station's morning show), even if working with journalists is foreign to you. Be willing to jump into social media marketing with both feet, even if you don't know the difference between Instagram and Twitter.

Be willing to try your hand at public relations (like pitching a story to a trade journal or making an appearance on a local television station's morning show), even if working with journalists is foreign to you. Be willing to jump into social media marketing with both feet, even if you don't know the difference between Instagram and Twitter.

Being tactic-agnostic is all about being sharp but being willing to try new things and change your mind as the sales data and customer insights demonstrate what's working and what's not. But what do I mean, exactly, by "tactics?" In marketing, we should first be driven by a strategy. Let's imagine that your marketing strategy for the year is to focus significant energies and dollars on customers who spend more than a certain monetary threshold with your business on an annual basis (or on those whose average purchase with you is 30% larger than the overall average customer purchase at your company). Your strategy might involve a commitment to allocate significant attention and resources to creating meaningful, personalized, one-to-one, direct marketing/communications to these

VIP customers because you believe that if you succeed with these customers, your business will thrive. Your commitment might also involve a decision to relegate all other customers (non-VIPs) into a category of marketing where they hear from you regularly but only through mass-messaging (not personalized, one-to-one connections). Perhaps the VIPs are getting fancy gift packages in the mail, personal phone calls, event invitations and special offers, while the rest of your customer list is keeping in touch through mass emails, are being alerted to sales or coupons, and they see your meaningful and regular posts to social media channels (where they follow you and still feel connected, despite the fact that you don't have to put too much attention on communicating with them). This "one-to-one for the VIPs and mass-casual for the masses" approach is your strategy. But you have an entire menu of tactics from which to choose when it comes to *how* you'll market.

Common marketing tactics include:

- Radio commercials (of various lengths, on broadcast stations and on streaming services like Pandora and Spotify — I'm listening to my "Classical for Studying" station on Pandora as I write this book and I've heard a great many ads for brands that have left strong impressions!)

- Television commercials (on major networks and on cable stations)

- Direct mail (postcards, letters, brochures, gift baskets — anything you can physically mail to a customer)

- Telephone outreach

- Email marketing

- Video (and display advertising on video services, like YouTube)

- Public/media relations

- Social media content creation and paid advertising

- Content marketing (blog posts, books, white papers, etc.)

- Website enhancements and search engine optimization (SEO) to attract more visitors organically

- Paid search (pay-per-click ads like Google AdWords)

- Display advertising (banner ads)

- Community event sponsorships

- Skywriting (okay, just kidding about this one).

As you can see from this list, which is anything but comprehensive or exhaustive, no matter what your marketing strategy is, you have a lot of tactical choices. It's a veritable buffet of interesting options.

But where do you start?

I encourage you to start with what works well for other businesses, and that appears to fit your brand and strategy. It should also be what you've been avoiding because it makes you a little uncomfortable. The important tactic I was avoiding was video. For several years, my company did well by relying on other tactics (website, social media, great print materials, email), but I knew that telling my story via video could be powerful. I was finally convinced when my former assistant made a case I couldn't argue with; she said "Kate, people hire you because they feel an affinity for you. They're impressed by your thinking, your experience and your approach to the work. They believe in your business model. Every time you talk to someone, there's a high likelihood they will engage in a formal relationship with your company. But you can't talk to everyone — there's only so much time for meetings. What would it look like if people already felt like they knew you and understood what you stand for and how you help your clients *before* they pick up the phone to say hello?"

The mere idea of taking days to plan a video shoot, sitting down in front of a producer and being under bright lights, as well as spending the money needed for shooting, editing, and the hair and makeup crew and more, felt overwhelming to me. It's a little hard to admit, but I was avoiding video tactics partially because I was pretty significantly overweight at the time and didn't feel good about putting myself — my body — in front of a camera. If you're a business owner, thought leader or corporate executive who has a compelling story to tell (on camera) to your constituents, perhaps you can relate a little bit; maybe you're introverted or you have a stutter or you hate listening to the sound of your own voice when it's recorded and played back. Perhaps all the fuss over makeup and lighting feels contrived to you. Whatever is holding you back, I encourage you to take the plunge. I was resistant in almost every way, but I forced myself to do the work. And it worked. I'm proud of the first few videos we created with the outstanding team at Focus Media Services, and those videos have literally changed my business and the conversations I have with new prospects. I received a Fortune 500 lead within 24 hours of sharing the videos on social media, and, even years later, nearly all new clients and prospects mention the videos during our first few interactions. The financial ROI has been remarkable.

In Chapter 2, we explored the importance of storytelling. Marketing tactics are the vehicles or "channels" through which you deliver that story to the world. It's vital that you start thinking about which channels are right for your brand and your customers.

Time and again, I have seen clients, and brands have business breakthroughs when they tried new things — new marketing tactics that were foreign to them but appealing to their customers. Tackle the new tactics one at a time. Not long ago, a renowned law firm contacted us about replacing their outdated website with a site that was visually compelling, told a powerful story, was well positioned to attract the right keyword searches on Google and elsewhere, and engaged visitors long enough and in enough ways to move them from merely "interested" to ready to make a call or fill out an inquiry form. This new website was one simple tactic that exponentially grew their sphere of influence. Today, the number of people who know about them and are considering hiring them has doubled. One tactic. On the heels of that success, they tried their hand at public relations — at proactively working with the media to help clarify their clients' side of the story for a major class action lawsuit. Working with reporters was new and uncomfortable for these lawyers, but they were successfully able to shift sentiments and clarify the facts, controlling the narrative about a high-stakes case that was pending. One tactic. And again, in the end, they generated vital, measurable results.

Time and again, I have seen clients, and brands have business breakthroughs when they tried new things — new marketing tactics that were foreign to them but appealing to their customers.

It's important not just to *choose* promising tactics, but also to be creative and smart about your execution of those tactics. When I worked for the graduate business school, I wanted to take advantage of the "Football-Game-That-Shall-Not-Be -Named-Due-to-Trademark-Laws" season — it was a time when mid-career professionals of both genders were tuning into television and consuming a great deal of media (articles, videos, etc.) about the teams and the game. My target customers were coming out in droves for the football frenzy, and I wanted my employer's brand to be there in the midst of it all. Thanks to some sharp thinking on the part of my media buyer at the time, we were able to do a "homepage take-over" with ESPNChicago.com the Monday immediately following the game. This meant that millions of readers who were giving their full attention to the sports channel's content were bombarded with messages and images about our MBA program — every single pixel of ad space on the homepage was filled with our branding. Visits to our website went through the roof, and our admissions team received a flood of new inquiries. Again, one tactic with outstanding results.

What one tactic are you willing to try this month? If you're really pressed for time or energy, identify a tactic that shows evidence of major impact despite how easy it might be to execute. A great example of a low-commitment, high-impact marketing tactic is advertising on streaming radio like Pandora. You can write a script, have a graphic designer make one banner ad, tell Pandora what kind of voice and music you're looking for and what kind of customers you want to target, and the campaign comes together like magic. Streaming services can serve up ads in highly targeted ways (by gender, geography and more), and campaigns can be short and executed on a budget. Try it out and see what kind of word-of-mouth reports you get about "I heard the radio spot!" and, of course, measure the website traffic referred to you by virtue of the Pandora display ad. (I should mention that if your website doesn't currently have analytics built in — so you can monitor and measure trends about what content is valued and who is visiting — you need to set that up immediately. Like most companies, we use Google Analytics.) Marketing should be measured, and the behaviors of your site visitors will tell you a great deal if you take the time to look at the data.

A WORD ABOUT PHOTOGRAPHY: INVESTING IN THE PERFECT IMAGES FOR YOUR BRAND

Before you start designing new brochures, website content, a white paper, internet banner ads or anything else, get honest about the quality and variety of your photography collection. Invest in quality photography, and you will never regret it. I have a client that manufactures office furniture, and they wanted their marketing materials to look like the beautiful catalogs produced by their Swedish competitor. They were wise to understand that stepping up to that challenge had very little to do with product innovations or graphic design — they already had great products and access to great designers. They needed outstanding new photography, so they did the work to produce it. Quality photography is especially important when selling products online (through your website, on Amazon, etc.), as images can make or break your listings. Just as people judge a book by its cover, they will judge whether your product is worth buying based on its photo. Testing your images is also important — try out which is more effective: showing the product by itself or showing the product being used by a person/model. It's fascinating how small changes can affect sales.

Invest in quality photography, and you will never regret it.

But what if you sell professional services? Or if you're a one-man or one-woman show? In some ways, photography is even more important for you! People want to assess whether they think you're approachable, friendly, strong, classy, professional, experienced, etc. Photography helps them do it. It's a big hurdle to convince someone to make a first appointment with a doctor, lawyer or management consultant. It's hard to convince a meeting planner to hire a highly paid speaker. But those professionals who have solid photography (and a variety of it) on their websites and elsewhere are outperforming (and out-earning) their competitors. Ask yourself: *Are the photos on our/my website as impressive as the actual services and products we offer?* If the answer is no, start planning your photo shoot. (Wondering how often I shoot new photos for my websites? At least every three years, I produce a collection of photos to keep things fresh — new colors, new props, new clients, new activities being portrayed. I also try to produce new headshots every year. It's awkward to meet someone at a conference and not have them recognize you because you look nothing like the photo on your LinkedIn profile or on your website!)

BELIEVE IN THE POWER OF GRASSROOTS INITIATIVES

Sometimes, the most impactful business results are generated by small investments, simple ideas and grassroots initiatives. Here are just two examples to spark your thinking:

1. I was planning a major market research study for an elite university and needed to recruit high school students and their parents for focus groups in regions where I had no experience placing advertising or knew virtually no one. Dallas was going to be my big challenge. But a tiny investment in social media ads, some strategic favor asking and a fruit basket got us our focus group participants (and resulted in so much demand that we had a waiting list!). I designed and ran targeted ads on Instagram and Facebook, which drove people to information and an RSVP form on our website, and I spent maybe $150 on these ads. My research associate happens to have a cousin who lives in the area of Dallas where we were headed, so we asked Lynn if she could help us. Boy, did she ever! She contacted teachers and

guidance counselors at local high schools and asked her own kids and other parents to spread the word. The RSVPs poured in. Word-of-mouth doesn't always happen accidentally — sometimes it happens because you asked for it. In the end, we treated Lynn to lunch while we were in Dallas and sent a giant Edible Arrangement (chocolate-dipped fruit) to her and her family after our successful initiative. Grassroots, golden results.

Word-of-mouth doesn't always happen accidentally — sometimes it happens because you asked for it.

---

2. A colleague of mine used to work for a company that served the legal market — lawyers and law firms were their target customers. One of their most successful marketing programs was a grassroots campaign that involved, as irony would have it, actual grass. Her company sponsored a hole at every local bar association's golf outing. Sales representatives from her company would meet and greet the lawyers in a non-selling situation. The relationships they formed on those golf courses and in those club houses generated significant and long-term business. Making that kind of personal connection goes a long way in building trust with prospects. Without trust, you're not going to get the sale.

CHOOSE MARKETING METHODS WITH VALUE, MEANING AND CONNECTION

A journalist recently asked me "What marketing methods are most effective and profitable?" As business owners, leaders or rising stars who are reading this book, you may be wondering the same. So I'll tell you what I told him.

I'd argue the most effective and profitable methods are the ones that create connection and meaning with the customer, offer clear value to the customer, and are based on data (customer insights that can be gained in various ways, including smart market research). There's no such thing as a marketing tactic that works in every industry or for every target market. There will always be "popular" or new tactics to explore, but it's foolish to jump on the bandwagon with new tactics without a clear understanding of how or if they will work for you. When smartphones were rising in popularity, and mobile app development was in its infancy, clients would tell me "We need an app!" And I would ask them who the app was for, what problem it would solve, and how it would create a meaningful experience for the customer. Ninety-nine percent of clients had no idea what they wanted this "tactic du jour" to do for their customers or their bottom line. They just felt like they *had* to get in the game. In truth, they were wasting time and money getting wrapped up in a technology or a tactic as a distracting "shiny new object" instead of getting clear on how a tool like a mobile app might serve the strategy they already had in place.

The most effective and profitable methods are the ones that create connection and meaning with the customer, offer clear value to the customer, and are based on data.

Smart business owners, executives and marketers have learned to be what I call "strategy-religious and tactic-agnostic" (*Think Like a Marketer* Principle #3), choosing only the tactics that align to an overall strategy based on data and proof and experience. You can learn to think this way, too. Interestingly, marketing decision makers also often dismiss "old-school" tactics, thinking they are too "out of date," expensive or time-consuming. Direct mail is a great example, and I'll explore this tactic in greater depth later in this chapter. So many marketing leaders, business owners or other proxies for formal marketers have reallocated their direct mail budgets even though their own data often shows it is their most effective tactic — driving

THINK LIKE A MARKETER
5 PRINCIPLES TO GUIDE YOU

Thinking like a marketer requires that you:

1. Communicate for connection and meaning, not just to transact sales

2. Live and die by your customer insights

3. Market in a way that's strategy-religious and tactic-agnostic

4. Create cultures and processes that align with your brand

5. Do everything in service of maintaining a virtuous cycle of creating value for the customer while capturing value for you.

the most leads, converting the most customers, doing the most to measurably build their brand or elevate their Net Promoter Score (NPS — see "The Brands and Businesses I Can't Stop Talking About" in Chapter 1 for a brief discussion of NPS measurements). Paper and postage are NOT expensive so long as what you invest into it is returned to you exponentially through new sales and business.

I believe that choosing the right tactics comes back to the right initial mindset — being clear and committing to the 5 principles, outlined again on the facing page for reference and reinforcement. When business professionals at every level and in every industry can learn to "think like marketers," the right tactical choices will naturally follow.

Has your willingness to try new tactics ever driven a compelling new strategy in your business?

Has your willingness to try new tactics ever driven a compelling new strategy in your business? Tactics should follow your established strategies, but sometimes it works the other way around. Sometimes the tactical tests can spawn new or refined strategies. Let me share an example. A social services agency with which I collaborate wanted to move get out of a rut when it came to communicating with people who were new to their mailing list or inner circle. They wanted to get past the desperate status quo of "join another list" or "please donate now." They knew there should be other ways to say "hello" or "thank you," but were stuck in old habits. In thinking through the tactics they could pursue and the messages they wanted to convey, they realized they lacked a "welcome strategy." They had no culture or thoughtful processes in place for how they said hello to (and got to know) their newest constituents. New people simply were lumped into a general mailing list, regardless of how they'd met or who they were. What started out as a conversation I was having with this nonprofit organization's marketers and leaders about how to improve their email messages became a truly innovative new strategy this agency now calls the Welcome Strategy. They initially thought they needed some new words or pictures (tactical elements) when what they needed first was a new way to think about the entire process. In your own work, be open to the possibility that the tactics might lead you back to a stronger strategy.

But let's talk about tactics some more. As for what tactics are "hot" right now, and what I'm seeing work well for my clients and others? Here are a few examples:

- For consultants, coaches, physicians, lawyers and other solopreneurs, writing a book is a major gateway to new opportunities (see Chapter 7). The business book is a powerful marketing tactic when deployed effectively. Thoughtful podcasts and quote-worthy blogs also elevate brands and create demand while building celebrity.

- For retail businesses, having a sense of voice and personality is everything. (And the voice and personality you convey is part and parcel to your stories of meaningful difference, which we explored in Chapter 2.) For retail businesses that gain and lose customers in an instant, long-term success is about connecting emotionally. Take Zulily, for example. They "celebrate" every purchase by sending a Facebook Messenger note, splashing the website with something like "Congratulations! You have great taste!" and even shipping their products in colorful packaging that continues the emotional high and sense of celebration.

- And as we explored in Chapter 3, being truly innovative about how to provide "sampling" opportunities can be a game changer for B2B and B2C companies alike. Not sure how to let customers of construction equipment or banking services "test out" your quality and experience? Get your people in a room and brainstorm about it. Remember, there are sampling strategies for every industry, and those strategies will present you with fresh new marketing tactics to test and master.

DIFFERENT TACTICS FOR DIFFERENT "FRONT DOORS"

Have you ever taken the time to think about how you welcome clients or customers into a relationship with your company — how they show up at your proverbial front door to create a relationship or buy a product? When they show up, do you welcome them with the hospitality they deserve?

In this spirit of "hello and welcome," one of the unique and vital challenges I have recently posed to some of my clients is the one I call the "front doors challenge." What are all the metaphorical doors through which people enter a relationship with your company? Perhaps it looks a little something like this ...

Door 1 – They see a Facebook ad and click on it to buy a product.

Door 2 – They come with an existing client to a special event you're hosting.

Door 3 – They sign up for your newsletter by visiting your website and filling out a form.

Door 4 – They stay somewhat anonymous but follow your brand on Twitter.

Does your company have a welcome strategy and a communications strategy for each of these distinct doors? Have you ever given any thought to how different marketing tactics might be more effective for some doors than for others? (For example, might you consider more digital/online marketing tactics for customers whose initial connection to your brand took place online but consider face-to-face interactions, direct mail or phone outreach for customers who arrived at a more physical "front door" — such as your office or retail space or a special event you were hosting?) How people initially engage with you might be an indicator of how they want to engage in the future, what they need from you and how serious they are about their connection to your business.

DON'T FORGET THE "TRIED AND TRUE" TACTICS: DIRECT MAIL AS A CASE IN POINT

I'd like to delve into one type of marketing tactic to demonstrate the quality of thought and planning that should go into your selection and execution of marketing tactics in general. Let's talk about direct mail — the letters, brochures, flyers, postcards, catalogs, booklets and even gift baskets that brands produce and ship straight to a prospect or customer's home or office. This chapter is all about trying new things when it comes to marketing tactics, and direct mail is an interesting case in point because it's a tried-and-true, old-fashioned marketing tactic that might still be a new approach for you.

Direct Mail is Anything But Dead

If you could invest your marketing budget in a tactic that would yield a return on investment (ROI) of 1,245%, you would. And if you could get your customers to spend 28% more with your company, of course, you would. Because you're a smart professional (and a newly minted *Think Like a Marketer* acolyte!), and you are dedicated to generating profitable growth.

So, why aren't you executing smart, targeted direct mail campaigns for your brands?

Wait ... let me guess. Because "direct mail is dead." It's not trendy anymore. Digital advertising seems so much more measurable, and it's what your CEO wants you to focus on. Your colleagues consider digital advertising "free" (because the volume of email deployments you generate don't hit an expense budget per se), but what's the price of having customers opt out when they feel they are being pummeled with digital messages?

I've heard it all before from the biggest brands and the smartest marketers, founders and C-suite leaders. But I'm telling you that direct mail is *anything* but dead; that the advent of innovative and effective channels like social media advertising and retargeting (i.e., automatically serving up ads — here, there and everywhere — about your company to people who have visited your website) does not excuse you from executing tried-and-true tactics like direct mail. The savviest marketers and most successful companies are eating your lunch when it comes to direct mail strategy.

Direct mail, despite it not being new or particularly "high tech," is a tactic that generates huge results for individuals and corporations that use it effectively. A few tidbits on direct mail results:

- **1,245% ROI.** According to our friends at Modern Postcard (a firm we use for a great deal of our printing needs), each dollar spent on direct mail yields, on average, a return on investment of $12.45. Compare this to the average ROI of non-direct-mail advertising, which is typically $5.29. So, when executed well, direct mail can produce more than double the results produced by some of your other marketing tactics. For some companies, a doubling of results might mean millions in sales, hundreds or thousands of new customers or clients, or significant gains in their stock price. Yet, some of the hardest working marketing leaders in America are dismissing direct mail as "too expensive," "passé," or "not efficient enough."

- **Customers spend more and spend more often.** A recent United States Postal Service (USPS) study also revealed that direct mail recipients purchase 28% more items and spend 28% more money than recipients of other types of advertising. Plus, more than 60% of direct mail recipients were influenced to visit a promoted website with the biggest influence on first-time buyers.

- **Customers are paying attention.** Why does direct mail often get such great results? Because no one gets meaningful physical mail anymore. So when you *do* get mail (at home or at the office), it's special — you actually open it. Email has become the new junk mail. While my clients are scrambling to increase the open rates of their mass email distributions from 18% to 30%, I sometimes have to remind them about the "open rate" for direct mail. A staggering 98% of "snail mail" is looked at and sorted on the very day it arrives. (And younger customers — Millennials and Gen Z — are even more apt to pay attention to direct mail than their older counterparts.)

No one gets meaningful physical mail anymore. So when you *do* get mail (at home or at the office), it's special — you actually open it.

Keys to a Successful Direct Mail Effort

While direct mail, when executed flawlessly, can help you achieve significant brand and direct response gains, it's not as easy as slapping your logo on a postcard and sending it out into the universe. To generate great results, a direct mail campaign must be firing on all cylinders. Before you release your next batch of art files to your favorite printer for your next mailing project, be sure to check out my Bonus Chapter on Direct Mail at SilverTreeCommunications.com/ DM. The following considerations are explored in greater detail in the Bonus Chapter.

1. **Strategy.** What are you trying to convey and what do you want the customer to do? The quickest way for a direct mail project to fail is for the strategy to be weak.

2. **The list.** Check out Chapter 5, where I explore list development and management at length. But remember that, like many other marketing tactics, most direct mail projects fall apart at the level of the list. No matter how amazing your brochure is, sending it to the wrong people (or not being able to get it delivered at all) can be disastrous and expensive.

3. **Message and creative.** You must say the right things, say enough, but not say too much. You've only got a matter of seconds from the time someone picks up the direct mail piece before she decides whether to act on it, set it aside, share it with someone else or trash it.

4. **Personalization and integration of tactics.** What has replaced static messaging is an innovative approach to marketing that can make use of personalized website URLs (PURLs) and combinations of variable data messaging (people love to see their name!) that is delivered via email as well as in the traditional mailbox. I was conducting some market research in Silicon Valley with some truly bright teenagers who were telling me about their college selection experience, and one of them told a story about variable data messaging that's too good not to share with you.

You've probably seen run-of-the-mill variable data direct mail, like a postcard that has your name incorporated into the design and that even has your company's logo or a sentence about something somewhat unique (like "It was great to meet you at the Business Marketing Association conference last month in Chicago!"). But when I asked these high school juniors to tell me about the "very best" college marketing they'd seen, one girl raised her hand and nearly shouted, "One university sent me a poster for my locker that had cool photos and my name. And get this ... the design in the background of the photo collage included a paragraph from *the application essay I had written for them*!!!" (That, my friends, is smart execution of variable data printing.)

When it comes to direct mail, there are many ways to be targeted and personal. And in a world where children expect the ad-server on their tablet device not to show them ads for video games they already own and where websites remind us that we've been meaning to buy those green throw pillows from Pier One, personalization matters more than ever, regardless of whether your marketing tactic is digital or traditional.

5. **Format, timing and sales follow through.** Direct mail, when done right, is hard because it's not just about the list, the message, the design and the strategy, but because it's also about smart timing (like getting the cadence of postcard wave mailings just right), about memorable and appropriate formats (like the college admissions team that mailed custom white boxes with Rubik's Cubes inside instead of sending another boring view book), and it's about sales follow through (like taking the time to train the sales team how to close the deals you are going to generate when customers receive their direct mail piece).

Direct mail, as you can see, isn't dead. But it also isn't *everything*. I would never suggest you put all your eggs in one basket. So, while I love direct mail, I'm unlikely to suggest you put 90% of your marketing budget against this tactic. (Unless you're like Bed, Bath & Beyond, whose now-famous blue and white sumo postcards with store coupon are perhaps the most ubiquitous and successful direct mail pieces in the nation.)

I suggest you start experimenting with direct mail and measure your results. But integrate your direct mail thoughtfully with other touch points, like social media, television, radio (streaming and broadcast), paid search and print advertising. And don't forget to read the *Think Like a Marketer* Bonus Chapter on Direct Mail, which includes predictions about the future of direct mail. Find it at SilverTreeCommunications.com/DM.

DIFFERENT OBJECTIVES, DIFFERENT TACTICS

I've made a case here for direct mail, but I've also argued that it's not everything. And that's true of every marketing tactic in playbook. Tactics should serve the strategy, and you need to be flexible about trying, testing and tweaking the tactics as you go. As you're thinking through the *messages* you want to share, the *customers* you want to reach and the *objectives* you want to achieve, be sure to align them with the *mediums/channels/tactics* you choose.

Tactics should serve the strategy, and you need to be flexible about trying, testing and tweaking the tactics as you go.

Regarding choosing the right tactic for the right objective or purpose, I happen to believe that direct mail is a powerful choice for direct

ASK YOURSELF ...

If your organization is like most, you're busy executing tactics because you've "always done it that way" or because "everyone else" is pursuing those tactics or because it just seems to make good common sense to be busy with promotional activities.

But ASK yourself ...

Do you know which tactics most efficiently drive revenue to your organization, which ones help customers understand and value you, and which ones are being ignored?

If you're writing blog posts on a regular basis, do your website metrics and other data prove or at least suggest that your blog posts are driving business?

(continued)

response marketing — it's a great *sales tool*. It can be powerfully applied to promote events, special offers, reduced prices, new services and products, and more. Direct mail is also great for brand marketing and time-bound offers or asks. I suggest it as a go-to tactic when you have the time, the budget and the creative chops, and when what you're trying to achieve involves measurable returns (short-term, such as when you're promoting a sale or event, or long-term, when you're introducing yourself or making the case for the value of your brand or your new products). I mail very little to my own clients (typically just special treats like "autographing pens" for the new authors in our publishing business), and I have never executed a direct mail campaign to prospects because our pipeline, thankfully, is pretty full already.

If you're looking to educate or entertain, I recommend video, blogs, podcasts or webinars. But think about whether you want people to read or experience your content, on demand on various electronic devices, a year from now. If you do, then direct mail isn't the right medium for the message because modern consumers toss paper as soon as they think they're done with it. (Well, okay, except for me. My office is home to mountains of paper. #INeedAnIntervention)

Whether you're a marketer, entrepreneur, corporate executive or a professional climbing the ladder, you probably have biases and preferences when it comes to the tactics or channels you use to promote your business. Perhaps you love email and think direct mail

(continued)

When you syndicate a blog post through LinkedIn Pulse, do you see a spike in the number of people who check out your personal profile and/or the number of visitors who come to your website?

When you conduct customer focus groups and surveys, do your most valued stake-holders remember your television commercials or your social media posts?

When you bring people or organizations into your sales funnel, do you find ways to quickly ask them how they heard about you and why they chose you? (And most importantly, if it's been more than nine months since anyone has indicated they saw your highway billboards or received your postcards in the mail, are those tactics on the chopping block for next quarter?)

is too expensive; you're betting on video but haven't tried streaming radio; you think telesales is too pushy and that banner ads are too passive. But the truth is that "it all depends." The channel should serve the business strategy. Be strategy-religious and tactic-agnostic.

Use these lessons about direct mail to guide your thinking as you explore the pros and cons of all the other tactics you might use for your business. You have a lot of options; there's no such thing as "cheap" or "expensive" (only effective or ineffective); and new tactics aren't necessarily better than old tactics — they're just new. In the end, my point is this — direct mail didn't die with the invention of email any more than the advent of the tablet computer obsoleted the cell phone. Whatever becomes the "new Instagram" in the social sphere won't likely kill Instagram, Twitter, SnapChat or Facebook. Today we have *more*: More channels to manage, more targeting methods to consider, more impressions to make before the customer sits up and takes notice. Being a great marketer is not about letting go of tried-and-true tactics just because something new came along. But it's also not about ignoring new channels when testing them out could be revolutionary for your brand. Marketing today (whether or not you have a formal marketing title or role) is not for the faint of heart. Why? Because it's a heavy workload to carry. It's no longer about "one tactic or the other" but about "one tactic *and* the other." There is more to understand, more to juggle, more to integrate and more to measure.

If your brand is like most, you need to be versed in every type of marketing tool in the toolkit. And then it's about matching the tactic with the messaging, at the right time and in the right way. No small order, but I believe you can master it.

THE FUTURE OF CHANNEL STRATEGY

How you allocate your resources to various different channels or tactics is often called "channel strategy," and when you've got a media mix with lots of different types of media, your approach is sometimes referred to as "omnichannel" marketing. The moral of the story is that the modern world is full of channels, many of which might offer incredible opportunities for you to create value for your customers and capture value back to the bottom line. Consider all the marketing channels, test your assumptions, measure everything you try and don't be afraid to venture into new waters. I predict that the most successful brands in the future will be the ones that:

- Are among the first to be seen and the first to be significant on new channels (perhaps mirroring the outrageous success Nike has had on Instagram Stories). *Big, pioneering tactical tests by big brands provide lessons for us all.*

- Only use gimmicks that tie logically and meaningfully to their brands in fun, memorable and share-worthy ways (like the humongous purple Adirondack chair in front of Julie's Park Café & Motel in Door County, WI, where you can seat an entire family for an epic selfie, or the world's largest American flag at Acuity Insurance, which measures 100 feet taller than the Statue of Liberty). *We live in a selfie nation and a connected world. What can you do to give your customers something to talk about?*

- Are nimble and aren't afraid to tweak, test, abandon and re-try (especially when marketing/selling online, where you can easily test content, images and pricing in real time). *Measure everything, experiment with affordable and simple ideas, and let the data (and ROI) guide you.*

. . . .

GETTING BACK TO THE PRINCIPLES

Marketing Tactics and the Think Like a Marketer *Principles*

When thinking about tactical decisions, it's easy to assume the only *Think Like a Marketer* principle that applies is Principle #3: Market in a way that's strategy-religious and tactic-agnostic. But tactical execution is where your entire mindset comes to bear; it's where your adherence to the other principles will be tested, too.

These other principles are also relevant:

Principle #1: Communicate for connection and meaning, not just to transact sales

If all your tactics focus on "buy now" or "call now" or "choose us," you'll do little more than just come off as desperate and uncaring. Balance the building of your brand and your customer relationships with your need to generate revenue.

Principle #2: Live and die by your customer insights

Whether it's email open rates, sales connected to one postcard design or another, or the input you receive on your annual customer/client satisfaction survey, the insights you gather — if you're paying close attention — will drive your tactical sales and marketing success.

Principle #4: Create cultures and processes that align with your brand

Your marketing messages and materials can, and sometimes should, address your company culture and your processes, too. I'm a loyal customer of Southwest Airlines, for many reasons, and I loved recently seeing a colorful mural (the height of the airport parking structure!) that acknowledged that their processes align with what matters to me when headed out on vacation. The larger-than-life message said something to the effect of "You look great in all those outfits! Go ahead and pack them all. #BagsFlyFree"

Principle #5: Do everything in service of maintaining a virtuous cycle of creating value for the customer while capturing value for you

Tactical marketing costs money — cold, hard cash and/or manpower. Invest in creating value for your customers by connecting with them, delighting them, sharing your stories and offering them something special, and you'll likely reap the rewards in the end. Remember that a great marketing tactic (and the right one for the moment) is not always the tactic *of* the moment (i.e., the new, trendy thing). Tried and true marketing channels (like television and direct mail) have worked well — across industries and with budgets of every size — for decades, and there are reasons why. Keep an open mind, and demand that your marketing tactics be dependable and powerful. You deserve nothing less.

07

SPEAKING OF GREAT MARKETING TACTICS, WRITE A BOOK!

A professional bio with the words "Author of ... " will always turn more heads.

One of the most natural evolutions my company has experienced was our expansion from a full-service brand marketing enterprise to a broader, more inclusive organization that includes a book publishing company as well. It only made sense for us to help clients produce revenue-generating and career-changing books. Whether you're a solopreneur or a leader in a large corporation, having a book can help build a brand. Books *tell* our stories and even *change* our stories. The right book can open doors for new business and for speaking engagements — these days, it's not unusual for me to hear clients refer to their book as the best "business card" they've ever printed. A well-written and well-marketed book can allow established professionals to reach a broader audience and redouble the impact of their mission. It expands the possibilities for passive revenue through royalties and it, quite simply, gives authors and organizations the credibility they seek. A professional bio with the words "Author of … " will always turn more heads.

Even in large organizations, a book (with one of its executives or notable thought leaders as its author) can create the opportunity for the corporate brand to be tied to the leader brand ("That's the company whose CEO wrote the book about … "). I remember cruising the aisles at the Container Store one day and discovering that their CEO, Kip Tindell, had written a book entitled *Uncontainable: How Passion, Commitment, and Conscious Capitalism® Built a Business Where Everyone Thrives*. The mere existence of that book changed the way I thought of the company, and it still does. For me, it was more than a great marketing tactic — it was a demonstration of *Think Like a Marketer* Principle #4: Create cultures and processes that align with your brand. I was intrigued and impressed.

I've been working with businesses — big and small, global and domestic — for more than two decades, and I've helped those organizations with every marketing and sales tactic in the playbook. And, when done well and leveraged fully, there is perhaps no tactic at any price point that comes even close to having the long-term brand-building and profit-generating impact as the "business book tactic." When we help professionals write and publish a book, we literally help businesses — pardon the pun — turn a new page.

5 THINGS TO KEEP IN MIND AS YOU'RE PLANNING AND WRITING YOUR BUSINESS BOOK

1. **If you think your business or your story doesn't lend itself to a book, you may be wrong.** Talk to someone you trust — in your industry or in the field of publishing — about what a book authored by you or your company might look like and

accomplish. Some of my very favorite book projects were with authors whose stories were unique — like Lee Quinn and Lewis Rudy's *On Your Own Terms*, a book about a process for making a business viable and attractive to new owners, and Wayne Sims's *Non-Profit/Pro-Growth*, a touching and instructive corporate history about an organization that changed thousands of lives by revolutionizing the foster care system.

2. **Think about *Think Like a Marketer* Principle #2: Live and die by your customer insights.** In short, let your customers demand what your book should be about. (And, yes, I'm practicing what I preach. This book contains the topics, stories and lessons that my clients and stakeholders told me they wanted to hear about.)

3. **There are many ways to write and publish a book, and not all are created equally.** Similarly, not all models or publishers are the right fit for you. Don't know how to "shop" for a publisher? (It's okay — very few people do.) Drop me a note at Kate@PublishWithSilverTree.com and ask for a copy of my "10 Questions to Ask Your Would-Be Publisher." I think you'll find it incredibly helpful as you navigate the process.

4. **It's okay to be nervous and skeptical — most first-time business authors are.** Consider *Think Like a Marketer* Principle #3: Market in a way that's strategy-religious and tactic-agnostic. Even if you've never considered writing a book, if it fits your strategy, give it serious thought. Don't feel like you have the writing chops? Hire a co-author or ghostwriter (more than 50% of books today are written that way). And, certainly, explore the game-changing option of hiring a book coach to help you from concept to completed manuscript.

5. **No matter how brilliant your book is, the cover design can make or break you.** So please, I implore you, don't design your

?? ASK YOURSELF ...

How could your first (or next) book create more value for your current customer/client base and/or a new segment of stakeholders? Is there something you find yourself explaining or teaching over and over — an element that your customers value immensely but that you're running out of time or energy to share in a one-to-one manner? Could that something be the topic for a book whose time has come? Finally, if you publish a book, how might it help you generate new streams of revenue, work differently or less, or elevate your credibility?

own cover with PowerPoint or hire a junior artist who has never designed a cover for an acclaimed business book. There's no such thing as a captivating book with a mediocre cover. Take a few minutes to visit SilverTreeCommunications.com and read the blog post, under the "Worth Sharing" tab, entitled "Go ahead ... judge a book by its cover!"

ALREADY WROTE A BOOK? TIME TO PUT IT TO BETTER USE

Whether your book was just released or has been in the marketplace for years, it's never too late to put it to better use. I tell my authors that a great book is not a piece of fresh fruit — it's not going to spoil if you don't get it to your readers before the end of the week. You can always create more value for new readers as you capture more value for yourself. Whether you need a stronger infrastructure to support the book (like thoughtful connections and the right mentions on social media or an outstanding Author Central profile on Amazon), a publicity plan to garner interest and build celebrity, or even a second edition of the book to introduce fresh ideas and jump-start new results, a book — if it has great content and a willing audience — can always do more for you and for your business.

> *Drop me a note at Kate@PublishWithSilverTree.com to let me know you'd like a copy of "Be Findable and Follow-Worthy Online," a set of 7 tips for book authors on how to make quick changes and enhancements online to improve the success of your book (and your business).*

THE FUTURE OF BUSINESS BOOKS AS A MARKETING TACTIC

"Books are magic," as my book coach always says. And they always will be. But will the world of publishing and the very way we use books as marketing tools change? *Absolutely.*

I predict that pretty soon, royalties from retail book sales will be the last thing on authors' minds. Authors, publicists and publishing companies will continue to innovate with B2B efforts (like the custom corporate editions of books that our clients sometimes produce for their biggest clients). Non-profits and associations (as well as foundations and other community-focused organizations) will use coffee table books and organizational histories to share their stories. Consulting practices (and even organizations like law firms and physician practices) will produce proprietary workbooks to help customers with everything from estate planning to nutrition tracking. And back-of-room sales during big events and speaking engagements will be one of just many venues where savvy authors create and capture significant value.

. . . .

GETTING BACK TO THE PRINCIPLES

Publishing a Book and the Think Like a Marketer Principles

When writing a book that serves a real business purpose, you've got to go further than just deciding to put pen to paper because you have something you want to say. Arguably, anyone who has had a full or busy career could write 35,000 words or more about some aspect of what they've learned, experienced or come to believe. But that doesn't mean there's an audience waiting for every book that could be written; if what you've learned, experienced and come to believe has *value* for others when presented through your book, then you're *truly thinking like a marketer*. If you're wondering whether writing and publishing a book might serve a valuable business purpose for you, think through these four principles.

Principle #1: Communicate for connection and meaning, not just to transact sales

Could writing a book help you to connect to others in a way that is meaningful for *them*? Could the book deepen conversations with clients and prospects, create a platform of followers who might ultimately become customer/client prospects and fans, and allow you to share insights that can inspire solutions for the business problems faced by your readers? If writing a book can be primarily about creating connection and meaning (not about transacting sales in terms of book royalties), keep considering it.

Principle # 2: Live and die by your customer insights

What does your customer data tell you about the needs and interests of the people you serve (the very same people who represent would-be readers of a future book you might write)? Are they struggling with topics you could explore in a book? Do they need a go-to resource or framework for their thinking, and are you the best person to write that book?

Principle #3: Market in a way that's strategy-religious and tactic-agnostic

If you've never written a business book to drive multiple streams of revenue at your company, then the idea of a book as a marketing tactic is new to you. It might seem as foreign as trying on a new language or a new religion. But could it fit your communications strategy? If your strategy is, for example, about doing more than just scratching the surface — but instead about providing deep insights and giving of your time and talents generously, and about collaborating in meaningful ways — the idea of a book may very well serve your strategy and serve it well.

Principle #5: Do everything in service of maintaining a virtuous cycle of creating value for the customer while capturing value for you

I'm a strong believer that a business book is the very definition of "the gift that keeps on giving." Months and years after it is published, it will continue to find new readers and new ways to help and inspire people and organizations in ways that only you and your book could have done. Be committed to the cycle of creating and capturing value — if your book creates value for its readers, it will ultimately open various opportunities for you that will surely generate value in return.

08

THE PITFALLS AND OPPORTUNITIES OF DO-IT-YOURSELF MARKETING

At the risk of making light of a revolution in the way businesses create and acquire everything from branded t-shirts to HTML email designs, I'm increasingly realizing there are enterprising, independent and budget-conscious business professionals who think "there's an app for that." In some ways, there is. Whether or not you have any marketing expertise, it's *possible* to create your own brochures, manage your own Google AdWords campaign or record your own podcast. But convenience comes with quality concerns.

At the outset of my career in marketing, you couldn't order business cards or pens bearing your company name with a simple click of a button. You couldn't pay someone on the other side of the ocean less than the U.S. minimum wage to design your book cover. You couldn't even find the name and phone number for someone at a national media outlet where you wanted to place advertising (like television commercials or magazine ads) — you had to rely on an agency with exclusive relationships and secretive commission structures.

LEARN FROM MY EXPERIENCE: THE PERILS OF SELF-SERVE MARKETING

I've tried out some of the do-it-yourself (DIY) marketing services and processes that have become so popular of late. Few live up to the hype, many waste more time than they save and most have ended in disaster.

I'm a huge fan of doing things differently — of supporting new business models (like how I abandoned the concept of taxi cabs the moment Uber came on the scene), of being more efficient and nimble, and of saving time and money. For those very reasons, I've tried out some of the do-it-yourself (DIY) marketing services and processes that have become so popular of late. Few live up to the hype, many waste more time than they save and most have ended in disaster. Here's the truth, and what you need to know (especially if you're a one-man or one-woman shop or if you wear many hats — because you don't have time to get it wrong):

- **Video.** We live in exciting times when it comes to video. We can shoot, edit and share/publish them from our smartphones. With social platforms, we can even produce on-the-spot events with the click of a button. Go ahead and use Facebook Live (or YouTube Live, Instagram Live Videos, SnapChat Live Stories, or Periscope) for "insider info" (like telling your fans that you and your company are on site at a major industry conference) or for fun (like showing your customers that your brand is sponsoring a charity 5K). When it comes to what you can shoot and edit for nonsynchronous viewing, you can produce your own low-production-value DIY videos for social media and email sharing, if that kind of authenticity and "down-home" simplicity fits your brand. But always ask yourself whether it *really* fits your brand. When it comes to vital media pieces for your website or high-stakes assets like a speaker sizzle reel, don't settle for anything less than a professionally produced and edited piece.

- **Custom specialty products.** With all due respect to CafePress and Vistaprint, your business probably deserves better. In a pinch, they can be useful resources for custom imprinted pens or t-shirts, mugs or hats, but with very few exceptions, I have found the quality of the products themselves and the quality of the imprinting (including whether a company logo is appropriately sized, placed or printed in the right color) always leaves me disappointed. Hire a specialty promotions broker; not only do they earn their commissions (which get paid by the vendor, not by you), they have volume-buying leverage because they have many clients (not just you) and can get you better quality for better prices than you could ever get on your own. Our Silver Tree branded apparel is incredible, and the gifts and supplies we keep on hand (like silver debossed custom journals for our clients and branded gift bags we use for just about everything) get compliments every time stakeholders see and touch them. If your go-to resource for pens, mugs, baseball caps and polo shirts won't send you samples in advance, won't engage a graphic designer to help modify artwork that's not quite right for the job or won't stand by the products if you're not happy, you need to get a new go-to guy or gal. I swear by Custom Specialty Promotions in Illinois, who have been serving and protecting my brand for more years than I can remember.

- **Creative design.** If you don't have someone in-house and on the payroll who can professionally design a PowerPoint template or presentation, a brochure, a banner ad or a flyer for your next event, don't go it alone. We have clients in a variety

of industries, but the savviest among them understand that if
a graphic designer would never attempt to practice medicine,
a physician ought not to attempt to practice graphic design. That
said, I *am* a fan of Canva, a DIY resource that's great for making
social media memes and the like; if you've already got the right
"ingredients" (a professionally designed logo, great photography, good writing), then Canva makes it easy to assemble those
pieces in a classy and polished way so you can do some of the
creative execution yourself. The art director at my companies
is an absolute genius, and I wouldn't dare produce so much as
a little poster for a book signing event without having her take
the lead. But I do make most of our social media memes myself
with Canva.

- **Media buying.** If you're not a professional media buyer,
  don't negotiate, plan and place your own advertising. Early in my
  career, I was maintaining relationships with sales reps from radio
  and television stations, newspapers, trade journals, websites and
  the like. I was trying to do my job as a marketing director while
  also learning to be a media buyer, which I can now acknowledge was insane. Whatever it is that you do for a living, I assure
  you that you don't have the time (or the money) to be a media
  buyer, too. Leave it to the experts. I have saved untold thousands
  of dollars for myself and my clients by entrusting their media
  buying to the good folks at Marketing Partnerships International
  in Chicago. They know what time of day your target audience is
  "tuned in," which media outlet has flexibility on pricing because
  of low inventory and how to score value-added exposure you
  never would have thought to ask for. As is the case with custom
  products brokers, media buyers earn their commissions honestly
  and fairly, and in the end you'll get more media exposure for
  less money.

- **Events and outreach.** Same story here, folks. If you're planning and executing a big event, hire the pros. If you're seeking
  publicity (i.e., attention from area media outlets and journalists),
  leave it to the media relations experts. Ditto for professional
  photography, models and voiceover talent. It's so, so easy to think
  you can do it all yourself and that it will save you money. But
  I could fill an entire book with just the stories I've seen as they
  relate to money and time wasted, and brands tarnished, because
  a DIY approach backfired.

- **Content marketing (like blogging).** If you're a great writer, an
  expert on your topic and know a little something about how to
  write for the web, you may be able to do this part well enough
  on your own. But don't be afraid to watch tutorials on making
  your blog posts search engine optimized (SEO) for better reach,
  or to hire an editor to give your drafts a final round of improvement before they are shared with the world. When it comes
  to high-stakes writing projects (like industry white papers) or
  editing projects (like editing your book), I recommend having
  a partner who has great talent and an eagle eye. One of my
  favorite clients is a healthcare giant that has skilled writers
  aplenty in its communications division, but they value my
  ability to take their data and turn it into compelling stories that
  have been engaging stakeholders, winning industry awards and
  improving patient safety across the nation. If you're like them
  and are a solid writer with deep subject-matter expertise, collaborating with a professional writer to bring your projects to life can
  be incredibly rewarding and fun.

- **Book publishing.** I can't deny my bias here (I do, after all, own
  a publishing company) but it's still fair to say that self-publishing,
  while it can be an incredibly educational experience, has a lot
  of pitfalls. Go ahead and try your hand at it if collaborative

publishing or traditional publishing aren't the right route for you, but don't settle for less than excellence. Hire amazing graphic designers, editors, book coaches and publicists — all with expertise in book publishing. Engage an editorial board and recruit a book launch team. Learn everything you need to know about pricing, distribution and promotion. Writing the book is the easy part; releasing the book is the beginning, not the end. Becoming an author takes a commitment that goes far beyond putting words on paper and sending it into the world.

Becoming an author takes a commitment that goes far beyond putting words on paper and sending it into the world.

- **Website design.** With just one exception, every non-designer and non-programmer I know who decided to buy into a "simple" build-it-yourself website platform ended up with an ugly, poorly performing and often broken website. But maintaining and updating your website regularly is absolutely something you should be able to do on your own, and intuitive processes inside content management systems like WordPress are making it easier each day to be "not a web guy" but still have a striking website that didn't and doesn't cost you a fortune.

- **Printing.** There are a lot of ways to get things printed these days, and not all are created equally. In the spirit of focusing on DIY options here, let me just say giving out handouts at a professional speaking engagement that were printed on your color inkjet printer on 20# paper is a poor reflection on your brand. Go ahead and pay the crazy fees at a convenient vendor like FedEx Office if you're in a hurry or, better yet, nurture a relationship with some small digital printing companies as well as large commercial printers, who can do fabulous work for you and who are efficient enough to be fair in their pricing. As for quick and convenient without breaking the bank, we've had a lot of luck with Modern Postcard, as I mentioned in the tactics chapter.

INTRODUCING DIY'S COUSIN, DIC (DO IT CHEAPLY)

Before I introduce you to DIC and start criticizing his character, let me first say that I am a strong believer in the agency model, in organizations and consultants that are essentially "talent aggregators" (finding you the right people for your projects) and in independent professionals who run their own businesses or freelance "on the side" to share their talents, one project at a time. My own marketing business got its start as a sort of "freelance" effort, the top-notch experts on my current team are all independent contractors who write their own metaphorical tickets, and the fact that I run a relatively low-overhead set of companies (no office lease, no baby grand piano in the lobby) means I can offer high-value services to my clients for a competitive price. That said, the rise in popularity of mass-available, internet-based creative agencies — where you can go to buy anything from a logo design experience to a blog post or an HTML email — has introduced complexity and confusion about pricing and quality. Do not confuse cheapness with convenience. Think of it like having Grubhub bring you a gourmet meal — there's nothing wrong with utilizing a convenient way to shop for and receive something delicious and high end. But sometimes, the same companies, agencies or websites delivering "the good stuff" are also peddling cheap garbage.

How do you know which agencies or websites can connect you with great talent? Do your homework, read the reviews, understand how talent is selected, ask to see samples or portfolios, and don't ever hire someone you've not spoken to via phone, video conference or in person. The best way to find reliable and high-quality marketing services is to ask other business professionals (in other departments at your company or perhaps those who own their own businesses) who they recommend. There's still nothing better than a referral from someone you trust.

Some of the most talented graphic designers and website program-mers are people I've met through my go-to-resource for talent, Creative Circle. In my experience, the people who are represented through this talent agency have portfolios that speak for themselves. They have been vetted and selected with the high standards of their clients in mind. But other agencies or aggregator websites, like Fiverr and Upwork, aren't so discriminating. A book author just told me that she received "three cover concepts!!" on Fiverr for just $15. (Well, she got what she paid for.) Today, Upwork offers dozens of graphic designers who will create a company or product logo for just $5, right alongside a featured graphic designer whose logo designs for major brands allow him to charge $10,000 or more. Clearly, these types of websites are full of proverbial apples *and* oranges. And it's too easy to give in to the urge to shop on price and choose a professional who is affordable or even downright cheap. Some of them, in fact, don't even deserve the description "professional."

I may never understand why some people are content with paying the same amount for a logo as they are for a latte. If they don't have any respect for their own brand and how it's created, introduced to the market and maintained over time, why would they expect customers to respect it either?

Do-It-Cheaply (DIC) marketing services are, in my opinion, one of the most damaging changes I've seen in my profession over the years.

People designing brochures for $20 are devaluing their own work, and they're teaching clients to think of marketing tactics as "products" that are entirely disconnected from the market research and insights, outstanding messaging, solid storytelling and innovative design, planning and distribution that allow such tactics to ultimately succeed. I may never understand why some people are content with paying the same amount for a logo as they are for a latte. If they don't have any respect for their own brand and how it's created, introduced to the market and maintained over time, why would they expect customers to respect it either?

How might you find affordable marketing support that's still top notch? Hire an intern from a local college or university, or engage a freelancer who is looking to build their portfolio by offering discounted services to people whose brands inspire them. Clearly, if you really do

ASK YOURSELF ...

When it comes to all the marketing work that needs to be done in service of your brand, it might seem enticing to do some of it yourself, as a way to save money or an attempt to save time or learn something new. But at what price?

ASK yourself ...

Whether it's the way you print your flyers, design your t-shirts or produce your industry white papers, are you currently resorting to any DIY or DIC marketing that's damaging your brand? Are you ultimately losing money in an attempt to save money, involve fewer people and move quickly?

have a friend who is a professional writer (and will edit your blogs) or a neighbor whose daughter is a photographer who will shoot your headshots in exchange for a $50 Visa gift card, give it a shot — be hopeful but realistically skeptical. Sometimes, you can score something amazing for a small investment, and I don't discourage you from trying. Be sure to budget time where you can't budget money, because when projects fall apart, and you have to start over, sometimes time is what you can afford least to lose. And remember that underpaying someone for their work often ends up hurting someone — you (because you don't get the quality you need) or them (because they aren't properly compensated for the value they have brought to your business). Or both.

Be sure to budget time where you can't budget money, because when projects fall apart, and you have to start over, sometimes time is what you can afford least to lose.

THE FUTURE OF DIY MARKETING

I don't have a crystal ball, but I feel pretty confident about my predictions when it comes to do-it-yourself and do-it-cheaply marketing services. I think the low-risk, low-skill inventions like Canva will continue to revolutionize the way we work. While other more high-involvement work, like recruiting the right people for focus groups, surveys or phone interviews, will be transformed by companies like User Interviews, which has a DIY platform that's user-friendly but also has outstanding project managers to help you along the way.

That right balance of convenience and ease for customers alongside valued-added services and counsel (such as you can get with a great custom products vendor, media buyer or event planner) will delight business professionals who have high standards and full schedules. As for the $5-a-logo guys, they will eventually go away because too many brands will get burned and the backlash will be significant. The websites and agencies that represent them will either go up-market to represent only truly talented professionals, or they'll go out of business.

GETTING BACK TO THE PRINCIPLES

DIY Marketing and the Think Like a Marketer Principles

Depending upon what you're trying to do quickly, cheaply and/or by yourself, many do-it-yourself or do-it-cheaply marketing processes or services can challenge you to think through all five of the *Think Like a Marketer* principles. I'd remind you to pay closest attention to the final two principles:

Principle #4: Create cultures and processes that align with your brand

If your brand is all about understated elegance, for example, resorting to processes and vendor decisions that result in garish, overstated materials that scream "home-made" is going to hurt you in the long run.

Principle #5: Do everything in service of maintaining a virtuous cycle of creating value for the customer while capturing value for you

Much DIY and DIC marketing is about saving money — about capturing or protecting more value for you. But don't do it at the expense of creating and maintaining value for the customer.

. . . .

09

BE KNOWN AND BE SEEN: NETWORKING

(But Not the Kind You Think)

My colleague Cathy Fyock has a special gift. She has the motivation to attend just enough events — to be *out there*, as it were — and to turn every meet-and-greet experience into new business for her book coaching practice. Cathy, you see, understands the unspoken truth about her prospective clients: No one puts "thinking about writing a book" on their LinkedIn profile, so the only way for her to find out about these would-be authors who need her help is to bump into them, in the real world where these conversations can come up naturally.

I'll be the first to admit ... I don't get out enough. I don't attend enough big conferences or assemblies of like-minded people who can inform or inspire me. Can you relate? I get a bit complacent about *being known and being seen* — out there in the real world, and away from the stacks of file folders and the pressing deadlines that are so evident in my day-to-day office cocoon. I need to invest in networking so people can know to invest in me. (But maybe not the kind of networking you're thinking of.)

I think I initially got turned off by the idea of "networking" because I was attending the wrong events and because I was going about it all wrong, missing the point that worthwhile networking was up to me (not the people who planned the events and charged me for a ticket). If you've ever attended a gathering that *is* actually called a "networking" event — where out-of-work professionals have stacks of resumes or where bubbly entrepreneurs rattle off elevator speeches while looking over your shoulder to see if they'd rather be talking to *that* guy — you might be turned off by the idea of networking, too. And if you've ever been to a chamber meeting, you probably know what it feels like to spend two hours fending off small business owners trying to sell you something you're not shopping for. These sub-optimal networking experiences in our pasts are probably why a lot of us don't get out enough. We can't find the perfect conference or event (at the right time and price point), or the last conference we attended was downright awful.

5 CLUES THAT AWFUL CONFERENCE YOU ATTENDED WAS YOUR OWN FAULT ...

We've all been there — the professional conference that feels like a waste of your time. You came, you saw, you yawned, and you conquered absolutely *nothing*.

But going back to the office without actionable new insights and valuable new connections is your fault — not the fault of those good-hearted professionals who stood up and gave presentations, or the unsung heroes who planned every last detail of the conference (down to the scavenger hunt in the exhibit hall and the 6:00 a.m. yoga class for conference goers).

Not long ago, I returned to the office after four days at the American Marketing Association's annual Symposium for the Marketing of Higher Education, and I came away feeling that:

1. It was well worth my time.

2. If I had attended that very same conference (same attendees, same presenters, same topics) 10 years ago, I would have thought it was lousy.

How is that?

"It's not you. It's me."

For a conference to be outstanding, you must be an outstanding attendee.

For a conference to be outstanding, you must be an outstanding attendee. You must participate, and not just show up to absorb knowledge like an empty vessel. Here are 5 clues that the "awful conference" you attended was your own fault.

Clue #1

When, within the first five minutes of a session, you realized it wasn't resonating for you, you decided to zone out to Facebook or email instead of getting off your tail and going elsewhere.

Professional conferences are not college classes. There will not be a quiz tomorrow, and no one is taking attendance. If you think a speaker is a bore or the material is not relevant to you, get up and go find another session that's better. Complaining later that the quality of the talks was sub-par when you could have chosen one of six other concurrent sessions is less than strategic (and a little short-sighted).

If you're a speaker at a conference, apply this lesson slightly differently by arriving early and staying late to connect with your audience.

Clue #2

You ate alone.

For each breakfast, you either ordered room service or inhaled a muffin on the escalator between the exhibit floor and your first educational session.

At lunch, you skipped out to check email or find a McDonald's because you "hate" conference food. (Seriously? Think like a marketer! I'm a vegetarian with Celiac disease. I typically eat Tic Tacs for lunch, but I still show up to the conference lunches because those beautiful round tables are the perfect environment to meet nine other people who can teach me something or become a valuable collaborator in the future.)

At dinner time, you met up with old friends who lived in New Orleans (or wherever you're conferencing), you had room service again or you ate alone at the hotel's lobby bar.

(But it's *definitely* that awful conference's fault you didn't meet anyone interesting all week. *Uh huh.*)

> *Tip: Read Keith Ferrazzi's* Never Eat Alone, *and commit to making some new friends.*

Clue #3

You skipped the opening-night reception and/or decided to drive/ fly home early rather than come to the final morning keynote.

The best opportunities for lengthy conversations (and free wine) often happen the night before the conference kicks off in earnest. It's a travesty to miss the social gatherings that precede the educational sessions.

And "getting a jump on traffic" when you should be showing up to hear the closing keynote (which is nearly always delivered by the conference's biggest rock star, as it was in 2015 at the AMA when University of Cincinnati's President Santa J. Ono mesmerized more than a thousand marketers with his "Donuts & Taylor Swift" presentation) is a huge mistake.

Clue #4

You showed up without a strategy and a plan.

"I want to learn something interesting" is not an actionable goal. Conference attendees who are active participants (and not passive learners) always come away with great results. Before going to a conference, you should set clear goals. Maybe you want to select 3-6 people on the attendee list with whom you must have a meaningful conversation before the week is over. Or maybe you want to meet at least one company on the exhibit floor who would be the perfect vendor for one of your top-5 projects next year. Or maybe you want to get to know the conference organizers so they'll recognize your name when they see you submit an abstract for a paper you want to deliver next year. Or maybe you want to give away some books (or have some books autographed by attendees you admire, as was the case when I loaded a suitcase with books for my first National Speakers Association conference so I could ask their authors to sign them — and they did!).

At the AMA (that conference that I could have thought was just so-so but ended up thinking was amazing), I met every one of my goals. Here's how:

- Months before the conference, I reached out to the four people who I was really hoping might be attending to ask if they'd be there and if we could schedule some time to meet. In every case, they were either going to be there (and I was able to schedule some time with them), or they weren't coming but my "Hey, will you be in Chicago this November?" email spurred a conversation that spurred business.

- I printed off the conference attendee list when it was sent to us (all 1,400 names). Then I skimmed it and highlighted the names of all the people I wanted to try to meet, or at least follow up with afterward (e.g., "I see you were at AMA this week. I'm so sorry to have missed you. Any chance we could chat once you get settled back in at the office? The session on XYZ got me thinking about your organization and your need for blah-blah-blah. I have some ideas on how to help.").

- I handed out business cards shamelessly and asked, "So, what do you do for LMNOP University?" This is a simple and effective way to make valuable connections.

- Each night, I took the business cards I'd collected and scribbled notes on the back of them (like "sat next to her during the morning keynote — she's the one who shut down all the university publications that used inauthentic 'kid speak' to try to appeal to high school students"). Then I connected to each person on LinkedIn.

- I dressed comfortably (flat shoes, jeans or khakis, warm sweaters and layers), I hydrated with tons of water, and I kept my body happy enough to stay focused and alert. During summer or warm-venue conferences, I live in sundresses and sandals.

- I had meetings with current business partners, future business partners, former business partners, a former employee and some complete strangers. I laughed, and I learned, and I enjoyed every minute of it.

Clue #5

You didn't bother to learn the conference hashtag.

I don't advocate "live tweeting" to the degree that you are so busy playing with your phone that you aren't really processing what you are hearing, but I do know that when I'm periodically challenging myself to distill the conference contents into 280-character comments, I'm learning. And I'm sharing. If you don't garner at least 10 new Twitter followers during a professional conference, you're doing something wrong. Share the love; share the insights; make new connections.

* * *

"But Kate ... " you might say ... "Sometimes a conference really IS awful. The speakers are troglodytes. The material was elementary and out of date. The chicken was like rubber." But I say, it's still your fault.

?⁇ *ASK YOURSELF ...*

I think every business plan, annual strategic plan and personal development plan ought to contain some clear intentions about what business leaders will proactively do to "be known and be seen." It's too easy to decide we're too busy or that it's not in the budget. But if you go enough years without being seen, you'll become unknown in your industry.

ASK yourself ...

Are you doing enough to be "out there" — to create new relationships, to listen and observe, to be known and to be seen? And when you're unable to attend an important conference or gathering in your key marketplaces, who else or what else can be a proxy for you? Could your staff or your business partners or your book be on hand? Could you ensure that your satisfied clients are there, talking you up even in your absence?

In the end, attending a great conference is *less* about showing up to an event that is perfectly planned by others than it is about showing up with a perfect plan to make the most of the event. As long as the right people are in the building (e.g., industry leaders, your peers, possible collaborators or clients or vendors or future employers), it doesn't have to be a travesty if the educational sessions are weak.

There are *amazing* conferences in your future — because you'll make sure of it.

Attending a great conference is *less* about showing up to an event that is perfectly planned by others than it is about showing up with a perfect plan to make the most of the event.

THE FUTURE OF NETWORKING

My guess is that it doesn't look, walk, talk or quack like networking at all. I predict that high-tech innovations and high-touch efforts will continue to revolutionize networking experiences (like conference apps that get us out of our hotel rooms and into the next session by texting compelling reminders, and like the outstanding mentor program that the National Speakers Association implemented to help new attendees get involved and get incredible value from their first event). I suspect that more networkers will do what I do: drift in and out of associations and conferences, go to events every other year and even let memberships lapse and restart as needed. I also hope that we'll see more innovations in online networking that help spur real relationships. While I was planning my first presentation for NSA, I had the chance to participate in a Zoom video conference with dozens of other speakers, where we could see and hear each other, and where the comments being typed in the chat box were riotous and fun.

· ·

GETTING BACK TO THE PRINCIPLES

Networking and Visibility and the Think Like a Marketer *Principles*

Principle #1: Communicate for connection and meaning, not just to transact sales

Whether you're the director of operations or the founder, you represent your company brand when you get out there to "be known and be seen." And taking the time to communicate for connection and meaning says a lot about you as a professional and about your brand. Going to a conference with a plan to connect and with zero desperation about closing deals or transacting sales inevitably means you'll accomplish more than those guys who are frantically spouting off elevator speeches and telling polite but uncomfortable strangers how to buy their product or service.

Principle #2: Live and die by your customer insights

One of the best ways to know what customers think and care about is to get out there and chat with or observe those customers — or people who appear to be a lot like your target customers. Think of it as unstructured market research ... sometimes all you have to do is listen. Don't be afraid to hang out with your direct competitors when attending conferences and other events, too. They're often happy to share valuable insights with you. One of my favorite questions to ask of competitors (e.g., fellow marketing consultants or book publishers) is "What are you seeing among your clients lately — what's keeping them up at night and what has them really excited?"

· ·

10

TOOT YOUR OWN HORN

(Business Success is Not About Modesty)

The good news about some of the best companies in America is that they're being led by some truly humble people. But the bad news is that companies and people who are too humble are being forgotten in marketplaces where "tooting your own horn" has become a necessity. So at the risk of using a term that might become obsolete by the time you read this book, let's talk just briefly about the "humble brag," shall we?

Companies and people who are too humble are being forgotten in marketplaces where "tooting your own horn" has become a necessity.

Active, strategic self-promotion is vital to you and your business, but it should not be confused with simple bragging or meaningless acts of "look at me!" If you have a wonderful company, then you also have wonderful people (staff, donors, customers, patients, students, supporters, strategic business partners, clients, friends, fans) about whom you can brag. And by bragging about *them*, you subtly but meaningfully brag about yourself, too.

Let me share some examples of how to toot your company's horn by sharing love with stakeholders.

- **Little acts of gratitude on social media,** like "Follow Friday" (where you tag and thank this week's new Twitter, Facebook or Instagram followers), are simple to execute and have the deliberate but subtle impact of putting your brand's name into the news feed for sometimes thousands of followers. I also love when consultants and other professionals post a beautiful or interesting photo online with a mention of a client or prospect they're visiting (such as "Watching the sun dance on the Chicago River as I walk back to the train after an inspiring visit with XYZ Company, whose innovative new ABC product or service is sure to revolutionize the industry."). Tell people where you are, what you're doing and who you admire. Make it about *them*. The fact that it's coming from your social media account also makes it about you. No need to be arrogant. (Clearly, a corporate post that says "Just killed it at my pitch meeting with XYZ Company in Chicago. So excited that they think I'm the best vendor they've met so far," is about *you*. Go with the "Chicago River … revolutionize the industry" Tweet.) Brands that spend a lot of time saying "thank you" and celebrating others on social media do well. Brands that spend a lot of time saying "look at me" and "buy my stuff" are doomed to fail.

Brands that spend a lot of time saying "thank you" and celebrating others on social media do well. Brands that spend a lot of time saying "look at me" and "buy my stuff" are doomed to fail.

- **Offer a webinar, host a conference, or invite clients and customers for a social event.** Ever wondered why busy organizations make the time to develop big events? There are lots of good reasons, but one of them is that being able to say to your target market "Please join us at our upcoming conference on market research" is a really smart way to say "Did you know we're experts at market research? Maybe you should hire us or recommend us to someone who needs our services." And when you throw a great event, if it's truly impactful for the participants, *they'll* toot your horn for you.

- **Speak at a conference or sponsor one.** Be willing to submit a proposal for a professional development or industry event where you want to "be known and be seen" (the theme of the previous chapter). Getting accepted to speak or having your company logo splashed all over the conference signage as part of your sponsorship gives you countless opportunities to talk up this connection without it seeming like too much of a "brag." The same goes for applying for awards programs. (But, without going on a long tangent, let me say that many awards programs are profit-making ploys that have nothing to do with whether you deserve to be "honored" — as such, stick with awards programs affiliated with professional associations and not-for-profit organizations, and programs with judging panels filled with admirable, credible people.)

- **Be generous with your written words.** Write a sidebar or foreword for someone else's book (without charging a fee for it!), write an endorsement for their website or submit a glowing LinkedIn recommendation. If the people you're singing the praises of are well-regarded by others, your affiliation with them is a small way of tooting your *own* horn while deferring the accolades to them. Just today, I agreed to be a featured blogger for the Nason Group's experiment on empathy; I'm not charging for all the writing I'll do and the time I'll commit because I think the idea of "building empathy muscles" by actively practicing empathy is a worthwhile experiment. I'm also doing it because I know it will provide me exposure to some intriguing people I've not yet met (i.e., Nason Group clients and supporters), and the collaboration will give me a chance to brag about Shawn Nason and Michael Harper's forthcoming anthology on the power of empathy, which will be the second Nason Group book published by my firm, Silver Tree Publishing. *(See what I just did there?)* Understanding that there's value in generosity because it reflects well on you doesn't mean that the generosity isn't genuine. It just means it's also strategic, and that you have learned to make time for generosity in your busy life because it serves many purposes, altruistic and practical.

Understanding that there's value in generosity because it reflects well on you doesn't mean that the generosity isn't genuine. It just means it's also strategic, and that you have learned to make time for generosity in your busy life because it serves many purposes, altruistic and practical.

Remembering to "humble brag" about your work and your organization takes practice and requires authenticity. If you're destined to be a real success, learning to do this will feel a little uncomfortable at first. You don't *want* to brag. You just want to do good work for good people and organizations. But business success is not about being modest to the point of unnecessary self-deprecation or invisibility. It's about making the right connections and about hardwiring marketing objectives into everything you do. Being a capable "horn tooter" requires a mindset shift ... of getting accustomed to asking yourself, in busy moments, "How might what I am doing right this second be something I can share with the marketplace?" And "How might this news about my customers be something I can piggyback upon if I sing their praises publicly?"

Just don't overdo it, friends. No need to brag (even about your awesome clients) five times a day on social media, or to have so many case studies on your website that no one knows where to start. I've recently unfollowed some friends and business associates on social media because they are horn-tooting meme-aholics.

ASK YOURSELF ...

Tooting your own horn is a delicate dance. Too much, and you'll cause eyes to roll. Too little, and you'll attract no eyes at all.

ASK yourself ...

Are you doing enough to toot your own horn? Are you doing too much? Will you know, either way, before it's too late?

I'm tired of seeing shouty Canva artwork that basically says "Look at us! Aren't we awesome?" (without being thought-provoking, kind or share-worthy) and LinkedIn posts that offer no value to anyone, but simply say "This person gave me a testimonial for my book and thinks I'm brilliant" (while not bothering with a "thank you").

Always, always, always shine the light on your clients and customers, rather than on yourself. If some of that light illuminates you too, you'll have earned it.

Always, always, always shine the light on your clients and customers, rather than on yourself. If some of that light illuminates you too, you'll have earned it.

THE FUTURE OF SELF-PROMOTION

I'm glad to see we can begin to talk about the art of self-promotion. I found it refreshing when bestselling author and self-discipline expert Rory Vaden founded Brand Builders Group and explained that the work they do helps other experts to develop "celebrity." It's inspiring that we can talk about doing well by doing good for others and that we don't have to feel ashamed for building powerful businesses and brands if those businesses are making a meaningful, positive difference in the world.

The best self-promoters of the future will pay it forward to promote others without asking for any attention in return, like when I asked (while seated next to her on an airplane) Cindy Hyken, Chief Engagement Officer for acclaimed author and speaker Shep Hyken, if there was anything I could do to help support the launch of Shep's new book, *The Convenience Revolution*. Without hesitating, she said "We actually really like to support others. Do you have a card? Maybe we can help you with *your* book." Of course, I pre-ordered Shep's book immediately and can't wait to read it.

. . . .

GETTING BACK TO THE PRINCIPLES

Self-Promotion and the Think Like a Marketer Principles

Tooting your own horn and doing so in a thoughtful and measured way is just good business. It also helps you apply two of the *Think Like a Marketer* principles.

Principle #4: Create cultures and processes that align with your brand

Different brands will toot their own horns differently because "bragging" is all a matter of style and personality. Make sure your approach fits your brand.

Principle #5: Do everything in service of maintaining a virtuous cycle of creating value for the customer while capturing value for you

Customer value comes first when it comes to self-promotion. Talk about *them* as a way to talk about *yourself*.

. . . .

11

FORGET THE 4 PS OF MARKETING: IN SOME WAYS, DISTRIBUTION IS EVERYTHING

If you're a marketer, you've got plenty of opinions about the 4 Ps (and might subscribe to the 6 Ps or the 8 Ps). If you're not a marketer, you might be wondering what I'm talking about! The classic "4 Ps" model of marketing posits that key marketing decisions hinge on:

- **Product** – what you're selling, be it a physical product or an intangible service

- **Price** – what you charge for it, what your profit margin looks like and whether there are different price levels or tiers, packages, etc.

- **Place** – where the product is available, such as in just one brick-and-mortar store, like a private boutique, or in a variety of big-box stores, or online through your website, or Amazon or elsewhere

- **Promotion** – how you talk about and promote your product through the various types of marketing tactics we've explored in this book.

Today, consumers want it all. I think the 4 Ps are just the foundation of what it takes to succeed in business. Shoppers (whether they're buying a pair of shoes or legal services for filing a trademark) want goods and intangibles *delivered* to them in new ways. How a product or service gets from the provider to the consumer matters more than ever. Let me share several examples to help you begin thinking about distribution — about delivery, logistics and how even professional services firms make themselves "available" to customers and clients in new ways. Feel free to skim through this list for examples that relate to your business or industry.

How a product or service gets from the provider to the consumer matters more than ever.

- There used to be just one process to consume legal services: You went to your lawyer's office. But over time, more legal consultation happened via phone and video conference. The forms and paperwork were literally *paper* or perhaps were sent to you via email. Now, clients are testing out new models for how legal services can be delivered. Every trademark application I've ever filed has been through Trademarkia.com, an incredibly customer-friendly website that acts as the "storefront" for an intellectual property law firm in California.

- How do you get your books? How did you get *this* book? Did Amazon send you a paperback and not charge you a penny in shipping fees because you have a Prime membership? Was it delivered via Whispernet as an e-book to your Kindle? Are you listening to it as an audiobook on a mobile app in your car? Did you pick it up off a shelf or table in a traditional bookstore or library? It's just one book, but there are so many ways it can be delivered to you. However this book made it to you, thank you for reading!

- Pizza. Everybody loves it, and it's been available in restaurants, via delivery and carryout for as long as we can remember. There can't possibly be any other way to deliver it, can there? Well, Domino's Pizza just announced "HotSpots," so you can have pizza delivered to you at popular locations that don't have traditional addresses or front doors — like parks and beaches.

- Why settle for just your pizza when it comes to delivery? Have the whole week's worth of groceries brought to your home. Our art director at Silver Tree is a city dweller, and she has her groceries delivered via Instacart. As her colleague, I once gave her a little spiff by adding money to her account to "treat" her to some free groceries. Same groceries, same grocery store, new delivery method — and for some consumers, the distribution method changes the game for them entirely.

- Who among you have tried Grubhub or other restaurant delivery services? Just as UPS and FedEx don't make the products they deliver to you, restaurants now have a way to engage a workforce of delivery drivers who don't formally work for them but who will deliver the delicious meals the restaurants whip up. This distribution innovation has provided a major lift in sales for a great many food outlets.

- Speaking of "lift," when you need one (from point A to point B), transportation network companies like Uber and Lyft have changed the game. They "deliver" a driver to you wherever you are (and their new real-time location services allow them to find your physical person standing on the curb, so they know exactly who/where you are — usually within minutes!). This is an innovation in delivery — I can have drivers come straight to me, rather than having to walk a block to stand at the official "cab stand" outside the train station. Can you imagine a public transit bus picking up passengers just anywhere, rather than at designated bus stops?

- Fashion is also experiencing revolutions in distribution, and you know that all too well if you've ever rented a special-occasion dress from Rent the Runway or signed up for a personal clothing subscription through a company like Stitch Fix. There was a time when no one among us could have imagined that our own bedroom, with natural lighting, could be the new "fitting room" for our favorite brands. These innovations aren't just for the ladies; my husband has been fitted for custom-made clothing by a J.Hilburn stylist who brought catalogs, fabric samples, shirts, pants, jackets and a measuring tape to our home.

- Amazon, of course, has changed the world in many ways, but their world-class revolution of distribution has perhaps been their greatest gift to society. For Prime members, most of what we buy is delivered to us with no shipping fees and the products we buy are processed and shipped typically on the same day we order them and are often on our front porches in just 2-3 days. My colleague, Barb, has a son who lives in Manhattan and he's discovered that it's cheaper for him to buy commodities (like toilet paper) from Amazon and have it delivered than it is to go to a local store.

- Even companies like mine are "delivering" services in new ways. I'm offering samples of my insights in this book, rather than exclusively through client engagements. Because I find that face-to-face interactions deepen understanding and impact, I conduct most of my client meetings via video conferencing (I use Zoom) rather than via telephone. It's had profound results for our stakeholders, and it has taught me to wear lipstick, all day, every day (which is, in and of itself around here, an "innovation").

- The revolution in distribution is challenging everyone to step up their game, especially brick-and-mortar stores. Heard on the radio here in Kenosha, WI, mere days ago: "Introducing same-day delivery from Target!"

- Even non-profits and children are getting into the game. Charities will let you register as a "virtual runner" for 5K fund-raisers, "delivering" the experience to you in new ways (and capturing value for themselves with ease). Girl Scouts are selling and delivering cookies in new ways, too. This year, I didn't have to wait for a middle schooler from my neighborhood to ring the doorbell (and incite riotous barking from my pack of four dogs); nieces and children of friends across the country were enterprising enough to set up online stores and online delivery, so being "local" no longer matters. As for lemonade stands in our subdivision, none have yet offered to deliver, but I suspect it's only a matter of time.

When it comes to building and maintaining a successful business, thinking like a marketer will take you a long way, especially if you're paying attention to the oft-forgotten and less-than-sexy marketing considerations, like distribution.

When it comes to building and maintaining a successful business, thinking like a marketer will take you a long way, especially if you're paying attention to the oft-forgotten and less-than-sexy marketing considerations, like distribution. Some companies feel products, customers and distribution (and what it costs) is everything.

I recently bought a t-shirt online from a client. I had no qualms about its $25 price tag but was incensed by the $8 shipping charge; ironically enough, had the t-shirt been listed as $33 with free shipping, I wouldn't have batted an eye. Why is that? Because we've become entitled when it comes to distribution (thank you, Amazon Prime!), and we might not even realize it. A 2018 survey by the National Retail Federation revealed that more than 60% of consumers expect that purchases made online will include free shipping.

Today, it's not enough to have an irresistible product or service at an irresistible price. *How* you deliver it can make or break you. Customers are demanding new levels of convenience, a flatter world and new definitions of "local," as well as new kinds of value, especially if those customers/clients are local and/or big spenders.

A WORD ABOUT THE FIFTH P: PACKAGING

When it comes to inventing products and services, it can sometimes feel like there's "no new thing under the sun." But sometimes, the "new thing" is the way the product or service is delivered or consumed. And this goes beyond distribution to considerations for packaging — the fifth P. Think about your last trip through the grocery store or a department store; did you see something on display that wasn't technically a new product but was packaged in a new way? I remember, years ago, thinking it was absolutely brilliant when drink mix brands (and I think it was Crystal Light who was first to move on this) began putting their flavored powders in little plastic tubes, so it was easy to flavor a bottle of water. *Why didn't I think of that?* And the current craze with comfortable mattresses in boxes small enough to drag up a flight of stairs without the need for two burly delivery guys? Also pretty brilliant.

??? ASK YOURSELF ...

Are there additional or alternate ways to deliver/distribute your products or services to some or all of your customers that would make them go wild with appreciation? Could a distribution change or improvement open up new avenues of business for you that could spark significant profitable growth?

THE RISE OF THE CITIZEN SALES FORCE

If you don't currently know someone (or a dozen someones) who serve as sales representatives, coaches, consultants (or a whole host of other job titles) for a multilevel marketing company (MLM), you surely live under a rock. I'm convinced that 20% of my social media friends are selling something through the MLM model — clothing, jewelry, packaged gourmet food, exercise programs, makeup and more. The model itself is a distribution channel — companies choosing to have their products sold at house parties, through other face-to-face interactions and on hundreds or thousands of microsites managed by independent contractors rather than distributing their products through one central e-commerce site or through big box stores or other retailers. For most of us who own or work in businesses of various sizes and in various industries, MLM distribution isn't the right fit. But given the sudden surge in popularity of companies following on the coattails of the original MLMs (like Mary Kay, Tupperware and Amway), I'd be remiss not to address direct sales reps for MLM companies in this book.

I suggest four considerations for direct sales professionals:

1. "Think like a marketer" so your income can expand beyond your current pool of friends and family (i.e., the people you have the most obvious ability to invite to a party or ask to host a party). Broadening your market will make it easier to accept when your sister or your best friend takes a pass on buying your products or on hosting a party. If what you're selling is truly valuable, there are plenty of customers out there. Find them; connect with them in meaningful ways and put the 5 Principles of this book to good use.

2. Think about your own distribution methods. Does your contract allow you to do innovative things that go beyond house parties and online sales? Can you participate in multi-vendor events at community gathering places? Can you do special demonstrations or sales via Facebook Live (or other live streaming services)? I'm the first to admit that I'm entirely burned out on LuLaRoe clothing, for a variety of reasons, but I still think one of the most innovative things I've ever seen a direct sales rep do was turn on the camera in her "showroom," pour a glass of wine, and invite dozens of us to ask questions, shop via video and even win real-time auctions for items with limited inventory. I logged in sure that I would bounce out in 30 seconds flat but stayed for at least 30 minutes and spent about $100.

3. Develop a culture and a communication style that is uniquely yours as a sales professional, but that doesn't run counter to the brand(s) you represent. My friend Angel sells Magnolia & Vine jewelry and adds a significant personal touch (and one that I love) by hand delivering my orders in beautiful gift bags (with hand-made gift tags, made by our friend Shannon), and inspecting every purchase with me to ensure I'm 100% satisfied.

4. Remember that speed is part of the service you deliver. I have a friend and neighbor who was my go-to resource for Mary Kay products, like the moisturizer I use every day. But selling Mary Kay wasn't her full-time venture, so she didn't carry a great deal of inventory in her house, and she only placed what she called her "big orders" every few months. That meant that by the time I realized it was time to order some more skincare or makeup products, I needed it within a matter of days or at most a couple of weeks, but sometimes had to wait months. So, despite her having a great location by virtue of living across the street from her customer, I ended up placing my next order with a friend's sister, who shipped the products to Wisconsin from Iowa and had them on my front porch three days later, in a beautiful branded box with a handwritten note. (Awesome distribution process vs. convenient location, and it's "distribution for the win!")

THE FUTURE OF DISTRIBUTION

No, it's not about drones! (Though that's fun to think about.) I predict that everyone from major retailers to mom-and-pop boutiques to physician offices will be challenged to innovate in the ways they "deliver" their products and services to the marketplace — that the organizations setting new standards and delighting customers in new ways will capture more of the market and will become increasingly difficult for the competition to catch.

· ·

GETTING BACK TO THE PRINCIPLES

Distribution and the Think Like a Marketer *Principles*

As you consider ways to innovate your distribution methods, think about your decisions in light of applying three of the *Think Like a Marketer* principles.

Principle #2: Live and die by your customer insights

What do you know about how people use or consume your products and services, and how they feel about the distribution options you offer them? Do you have data (or could you ask for it) about how distribution speed, convenience and cost is impacting their affinity and affection for your brand, their willingness to recommend your business, and how often and how much they spend with you?

Principle #4: Create cultures and processes that align with your brand

There are dozens of processes in every business that deserve scrutiny through a "think like a marketer" lens. Distribution may be the one that deserves your most urgent and thoughtful attention.

Principle #5: Do everything in service of maintaining a virtuous cycle of creating value for the customer while capturing value for you

In thinking about your distribution decisions, never lose sight of the create/capture imperative. Some distribution decisions (like building new warehouses or offering free shipping) can cost significant money for you in the short term. But what might the ROI look like? Does the distribution improvement you're considering create value for the customer? Does the model save/make money or offer a benefit so attractive to the customer that it will drive sales volume, so you capture more money in the long run?

. . . .

12

DON'T LET GOOD CUSTOMER SERVICE GO BAD

Being IN business is not enough. Being OPEN for business won't keep you from going out of business.

And yet, many business owners and leaders think that starting an enterprise or working diligently each day in one is enough. It's not enough. Ask your customers or clients if they really care how many hours you put in last week. They don't. What they care about is whether you care about them. They care about whether you are addressing their needs and wants with products, services and customer support in the way they expect. The only way to do this is to think like a marketer — to constantly put yourself in the shoes of the customer, to see and critique your brand through their eyes.

Ask your customers or clients if they really care how many hours you put in last week. They don't. What they care about is whether you care about them.

Customer service can be your competitive edge. It can also be your Achilles heel. Let's explore the possibilities of both.

My friend, Carrie, owns an insurance brokerage firm called Horizon Benefit Services. In an era of major healthcare legislation changes and a shrinking health insurance market, customer service — over and above her expertise in healthcare reform and employee benefits — is what differentiates and saves her. I'm convinced that if her business were to dramatically shift or even close as a result of industry changes, her customers would patronize anything her entrepreneurial heart cooked up next. She doesn't just deliver great customer service; she delivers devotion to her stakeholders. These days, that's rare indeed.

Think for a moment about the best customer service experiences you've ever had. Maybe a restaurant treated you like a celebrity on your birthday, or a veterinarian took your sick puppy — who needed 24/7 monitoring — on vacation with him, so she was under constant doctor's care. Maybe there's a utility company, telecomm firm or retail business that is always reachable via phone and live internet chat whenever you need them. Maybe they always have answers to your questions and solutions to your crises. Maybe your attorney, marketing consultant or accountant makes himself available to you when a pressing deadline leaves you desperate for expert counsel on the weekend.

Outstanding customer service is an extension of distribution — it's a way to deliver *value*. It's also a reflection of your brand, proof of your story and should be informed by customer insights.

Outstanding customer service is an extension of distribution — it's a way to deliver *value*. It's also a reflection of your brand, proof of your story and should be informed by customer insights. When's the last time you conducted a survey or other research effort to find out if the "customer service" you're delivering is delighting, disappointing or leaving no impression at all?

WHEN CONVENIENCE AND CONNECTION BECOME "TOO MUCH"

There's something you should know about customer service ... good intentions can go bad. An effort at offering convenience and connection might ultimately go too far, turning customers away and tarnishing your brand. Let me share just two examples of this.

Several years ago, I tried out my first fashion subscription service (a sort of VIP "club") by signing up for Adore Me, a company that sells bras and panties, sleepwear and loungewear. I could not have loved their products more. Buying something new each month was a decadent and exciting experience. I happily let them charge my debit card each month in exchange for getting to choose a new "set" (like pajama top and bottoms). But there came a point when I'd had enough of their clothes; I loved it all, but I simply didn't need anymore. So, I tried to shut off the subscription service and couldn't. You see, their processes appeared to be designed to handcuff customers into an ongoing commitment, far beyond the customer's interest. I called to turn off my membership and was told that I couldn't cancel in the period between when I'd placed an order and when it had arrived on my front porch. Then I put a reminder on my calendar and called them about a week later. I'd received my purchases and was ready to cancel. But they had just processed an automatic charge to my credit card for my next outfit. I asked if they could refund the money. *No.* Well, I didn't want to leave that money "on the table," as it were, so I ordered something else with my credit. But then I couldn't cancel because I was in that no-mans-land between order and delivery again. I finally discovered, about $300 later, the date on which I could cancel. I think I went through eight different steps and website screens, trying to say goodbye. I kept getting hit with different offers, like a chance to only buy four sets a year instead of 12, or a chance to turn off the automatic charge just for this month. I tried and tried and tried to get out of their stranglehold. Eventually, I was free. And now, here I am, with dresser drawers full of high-quality apparel from this company and feeling hard-pressed to say a single nice thing about them because — beyond the products, the promotions, the ease of purchase and so much more — their attempt at "customer service" turned them into stalkers and scammers (though, in their defense, that might never have been their intention). This was, for me, the ultimate case of "good customer service gone bad." I was more than disappointed; I was furious. Has something like this ever happened to you? Were you able to resist the urge to lambast the company on social media, or mention them in your new book?

Whether your business is a multi-million-dollar enterprise or you're a solo practitioner, it's always possible to blow it when it comes to customer service.

If you rub your customers the wrong way, get too pushy or don't deliver what they feel they have paid for (and then don't make it right through outstanding customer service), what might the fallout look like? Negative online reviews? Lost business? Social media backlash? Whether your business is a multi-million-dollar enterprise or you're a solo practitioner, it's always possible to blow it when it comes to customer service. Last year, I met a woman at a human resources conference, where a group of my book authors was hosting a book signing for their new anthology. I chatted briefly with the woman and traded business cards with her. A couple of weeks later, this unassuming HR professional turned out to be an overzealous sales-person, hell-bent on selling me skin care products I wasn't shopping for. I have no doubt that she "meant well" — that she thought she could create value for me if only I'd listen to her and give her my money. But meaning well is not enough. When communicating with customers and prospects, you must actually *do* well. Customer service gone awry can be the mortal blow for any business.

Meaning well is not enough. When communicating with customers and prospects, you must actually *do* well.

WHEN YOU MESS UP, STEP UP

No matter how hard you try, you and your business are going to have bad situations that require quick thinking and outstanding customer service. Sometimes, a misstep just requires a heartfelt apology. Other times, it requires generous refunds or more. But when you mess up in the eyes of your customer, it's always time to step up.

Let me tell you about a hotel that stepped up, and about the bed bug that turned me into a queen. I was at a high-end hotel in Dallas, preparing to conduct focus groups on behalf of a university client. Despite the hotel's stunning lobby, everything else was already falling a little short on day one. The sink in my wet bar leaked and I had a minor flood in the lower cabinet that required a call to engineering before I'd even unpacked. Also, I was carrying a lot of cash (incentives for focus group participants), but my in-room safe was broken. The help from hotel staff was lukewarm. The catering director, despite all of our previous meetings and signed contracts, still had the rooms set up incorrectly and had forgotten that we'd scheduled a walk-through with the audio-visual team. This hotel's every weakness was exposed.

I considered writing a blog post about the hotel's utter lack of hospitality, and the irony of it, but I was too tired, so I went to sleep. And in the morning, I found a bedbug on my sheets. I squished it between my fingers and cringed to see all the blood (presumably *my* blood).

I took a photo of the dead bedbug — brown and creepy and bloody against a stark white tissue — and went to the front desk where I got stares and whispers. I left a message on the catering director's cell phone. The front desk staff told me to go back to my room — that the catering director and a team of people from engineering were in my room, waiting for me. Suffice it to say that in the very moment when this hotel's team could have let things go from bad to worse, they stepped up. In a matter of minutes, my room was torn apart, and a manager in a suit showed up with a luggage cart and a keycard to a suite that was made for royalty. Hotel employees repacked all my belongings (including boxes of event handouts, gifts and more), told me that my new room was directly across the hall from the boardroom where I was conducting the focus groups, and urged me to get to the restaurant for brunch, to have my meeting with AV and to not worry about a thing. That brunch included mimosas, and it was free. Every other meal my colleague and I ate during our stay was free. My new suite had four rooms (two bathrooms!) and included a huge marble conference table, where we were able to set up everything for our event and to work more productively than at any other hotel we visited that year. The suite was replenished with champagne, fresh fruit, chocolates and flowers. The following day was my birthday, and the catering director became our personal concierge, recommending fun things we could do and see in celebration of my special day. She made our dinner reservations at a remarkable restaurant, and a hotel employee stayed after his scheduled shift to drive us there. Our business engagements were a huge success, and we ultimately had a good time, too. On day one, I was ready to write a negative blog or review.

Then I was ready to post a bloody bedbug photo to social media. My friends insisted I needed to file an online bedbug report (the kiss of death in the hotel industry). Then the hotel stepped up and did so in big ways. Now, I'd try staying there again. Making things right can be a powerful reflection of your brand personality.

Surely, this hotel lost money on us in the end. But how much *might* they have lost had they handled the situation differently? When you mess up or when things just happen (like a bedbug!), are you able to immediately do the right thing for the customer, even if it's hard, embarrassing or expensive? It's possible to lose perspective when trying to strike the right balance between caring for the customer and caring for the company and yourself.

You can have boundaries without being a jerk, and you can go above and beyond without sacrificing your success.

You can have boundaries without being a jerk (like saying "no" to a client who asks for the moon and isn't entitled to it), and you can go above and beyond without sacrificing your success (like when it's easy and affordable enough to make things right by issuing a refund, providing some extra perks or taking the time to really connect and hear your customer's concerns). Customer service is where you can do so much to *create* value that eventually *becomes* value for the bottom line.

DON'T ASK ... INVITE. DON'T JUST THANK ... CELEBRATE.

I believe there's a distinct difference between *asking* a customer (to buy your product, consider a contract, to spend time learning more about your business) and *inviting* a customer into a relationship with

??? ASK YOURSELF ...

Can you believe ... many companies, especially those that offer professional services, don't even have an articulated strategy or plan for delivering customer service?

ASK yourself ...

If budget and staffing were not an issue, what could and would you do to deliver the very best possible customer service to the people who know, love and support you? Have you conducted even a simple customer survey or other research effort recently to find out how your customers think you currently stack up when it comes to customer service?

you and your brand. Do you appreciate the difference? Are there ways you can welcome people rather than just selling to them?

I also believe in celebrating a purchase instead of just handing over a receipt. "Thank you" is a huge opportunity that eludes companies and leaders who don't *think like marketers*. We can all take a lesson from Zulily, who thanks you three times — first, with an on-screen celebration (including animated confetti) when you place your order, then a thank-you note via Facebook Messenger (if you've integrated your Zulily account with Facebook) and then with an email confirmation. When your package arrives in the mail, in a cheerful blue polybag with white flower designs, the "headline" on the bag says "Yay! Your fabulous find is inside. Tear here." That, my friends, is more than commerce. That's world-class customer service. That's congratulating the customer on being so fashionable and on acting fast to secure a deal before the inventory runs out.

THE FUTURE OF CUSTOMER SERVICE

Because so many companies are delivering such great customer service, the rest of us will be forced to step up or be marginalized. I predict the telephone will become the most powerful digital innovation of our time. What's old will become new again. Right now, the telephone is the most underused piece of "social media." If people start picking it up again and connecting in meaningful ways, powerful things will happen. Phone calls with customers can include video, too — I'm a Zoom lover as I mentioned; seeing your colleagues laugh and smile or grimace and ponder allows you to accomplish more in shorter periods of time. Our collegiate research in the past several years has shown that the customers of the future (Gen Z) hate email — they don't read it. It's lame. But they're surprised and flattered when someone calls and invites them to something. When someone imparts insight or a coupon code and does it in a very personal one-to-one way. We even heard from a young man in Silicon Valley — whose parents work in high tech and who arguably should be most "wowed" by the cutting edge and bored with "old-school" tools, like the telephone — that the very best action he's seen a college or university take in trying to recruit him was when an admissions manager called to wish him a happy birthday, to ask what his weekend plans were — all while not saying a word about application deadlines or campus tours. Take note, think-like-a-marketer friends! We're all obsessed with communicating with the "many" all at once (through mass email deployments, social media, direct mail, radio, television), but business success is often achieved one customer at a time.

We're all obsessed with communicating with the "many" all at once (through mass email deployments, social media, direct mail, radio, television), but business success is often achieved one customer at a time.

. . . .

GETTING BACK TO THE PRINCIPLES

Customer Service and the Think Like a Marketer *Principles*

All aspects of customer service — the good, the bad and the ugly — can use the entire 5 *Think Like a Marketer* principles. But there are two you should keep top of mind.

Principle #4: Create cultures and processes that align with your brand

I recently forgot several toiletries when traveling. I called the hotel's front desk to ask if there was a shop in the building where I could buy toothpaste, a razor and some shaving cream. "No, ma'am. We're sending someone to your room to give you some. How much do you need?" #Hospitality

Do your people exude an unflagging commitment to a culture that aligns with your brand? Do your processes go beyond "how to get things done" and rise to the level of outstanding customer service? Do some of your processes, like the fashion subscription horror story in this chapter, actually qualify as *bad* customer service?

Principle #5: Do everything in service of maintaining a virtuous cycle of creating value for the customer while capturing value for you

Great customer service is all about creating value for those you serve — in good times and bad, in predictable interactions and during unexpected moments. What customer service initiatives at your business are creating so much value for customers that they're directly driving profit back to the bottom line?

. . . .

13

A LITTLE MARKET RESEARCH GOES A LONG WAY

Sometimes, you don't know what you don't know. But it's high time you found out.

Sometimes, you don't know what you don't know. But it's high time you found out.

There are certainly some universal truths of marketing and business. I happen to think that one of the most vital truths is that the difference between breakthrough leadership and merely hopeful and hardworking leadership is data — that the businesses and people who succeed will be those driven by a mindset that the insights they seek can be acquired. It's about asking, asking often, asking in the right way and asking the right people.

IS THERE A REPORT FOR THAT?

Marketing professionals and non-marketing leaders alike — whether they work in a small non-profit or a Fortune 100 company — often have one thing in common: they have no idea how far a little research could take them.

Marketing professionals and non-marketing leaders alike — whether they work in a small non-profit or a Fortune 100 company — often have one thing in common: they have no idea how far a little research could take them.

Imagine you are the director of enrollment services (i.e., admissions) for a college where undergraduate enrollment has been slipping. Now, imagine how the future (and your blood pressure) might change if someone handed you a report that told you exactly what your prospective students think of your brochures, your website, the campus tour experience and your promotional videos. What if the report had a matrix of dos and don'ts for everything from website architecture to design styles to paper preferences among high school students in your target profile? And what if the report had 12 affordable, actionable recommendations that could turn around your enrollment problem before the start of the next academic year?

I, for one, imagine you'd love to get your hands on that report.

But maybe you don't work in higher education. Maybe you're thinking:

- *I own a small consulting firm, and I need to secure more speaking engagements, more clients and more repeat business. Do you have a report for that?*

- *Our company sells women's shoes, and we are trying to attract more young professionals to our store in downtown Milwaukee. Is there a report that will tell me how to do that?*

- *We are a business-to-business (B2B) company that provides roofing supplies to home builders. We are trying to determine whether to grow our business in its home region or to open offices and hire a sales force elsewhere. Is there a report for that?*

Yes, there's a report for *all* that … and more. You see, whether you sell widgets or consulting services, shingles or peep-toe pumps, the health of your business should not be left to chance. Why guess about the profile of the ideal customer, the packaging color that would turn heads and open wallets, or which intersection in Wichita offers the best opportunity for foot traffic into your next brick-and-mortar retail location?

If you're like most business professionals, you're smart and talented but wasting a lot of time and money on guesswork. You deploy direct-mail campaigns with language and offers that your copywriter thinks are interesting (brilliant even!); but unless you're selling your product or service to a target market of copywriters, it's probably about time you found out what your actual customers care about. You've probably developed products with features that the customers don't need and aren't willing to pay for. Why?

Why are we continuing to treat marketing communications like a crap shoot instead of harnessing the insights of the marketplace? In truth, marketing is as much science as it is art. And it's high time you quit finger painting like an amateur.

You need some "tough love" from someone who's been in your shoes as a marketing professional or business owner — someone who's not afraid to tell you where you've gone astray and how to get back on the straight and narrow path to increased revenues. Ask yourself this: "Why are we continuing to treat marketing communications like a crap shoot instead of harnessing the insights of the marketplace?" In truth, marketing is as much science as it is art. And it's high time you quit finger painting like an amateur.

SMALL INVESTMENTS, BIG RESULTS

But isn't market research expensive? Isn't it time-consuming? Won't a valuable effort to glean market insights distract you from finishing that series of banner ads or editing your annual report or preparing for the big industry trade show? Only if you partner with the wrong marketing strategists (the ones who leave you with a thick dusty binder full of ideas you can't afford to execute), or if the internal team leading your effort doesn't know how to get rich, unbiased insights.

Research comes in many forms, and I've conducted it all:

- Surveys (online and paper-based)
- Focus groups
- Interviews
- Structured observations
- Competitive scans

There have been projects that involved 3,500 participants and projects where the input of just eight people around a conference table allowed an organization to make meaningful and profitable pivots.

HOW TO GET STARTED

Finish the following sentence about your business: "If we only knew ... , we'd have more business than we could ever imagine." Discover what's in the "dot dot dot." *What's your ellipsis?* Don't know how to

make your product appeal to customers aged 18-25? Don't know
whether patients are more likely to schedule their annual mammo-
gram if you send a postcard or an email? Don't know whether your
Memorial Day Sale would attract more serious buyers for furniture if
you offered a 15% off coupon or a drawing for a free sofa?

Once you know what you *don't* know, you're ready to start investigating. And you don't have to go it alone. There are plenty of research
nerds like me who would be happy to help you find your way to the
data you seek.

Even the most strategic professionals (including formal marketers)
tend to lose sight of the value of a little research. (Yes, some
marketers need to be reminded to "think like a marketer!" I actually
remind myself every day.) And even if a market research initiative
is on your radar, you likely don't know where to start. What's more,
many organizations (even large ones) don't have anyone on staff with
expertise in focus group facilitation or survey instrument development. That's partially why so many easy-to-execute market research
initiatives never get started.

**Regardless of your industry or budget, the news is good. Business
intelligence is yours for the taking.**

Regardless of your industry or budget, the news is good. Business
intelligence is yours for the taking — get your hands on your
share, and begin reaping the business results. "Yes, there's a report
for that." And I'd be happy to write it for you. (Find me at Kate@
SilverTreeCommunications.com.)

??? ASK YOURSELF ...

Of the projects sitting on your desk right this very moment, which ones were you about to rush full-steam-ahead into without all the data and insights to guide you? Where are the holes in your knowledge? And how easy might it be to execute some research — with your customers, with people in the marketplace who look like your customers, with purchase influencers or with people who you have lost — to sharpen your next steps? How might every dollar spent on marketing research translate into $100 (or more!) added to the company's bottom line?

UNDERSTANDING YOUR AUDIENCE

Everything in business comes down to understanding the customers you serve. Market research is sometimes the best way to learn more about those customers and to connect with them directly. For my clients and me, market research is what keeps us humble and open-minded about target audiences. You see, every time we make lists of "what we think we know" about the customers and then test those assumptions through our research, a significant portion of those assumptions turn out to be wrong.

Here's just one fun example of an audience discovery that took me by surprise. I was in Southern California, speaking with high-talent, high-income high school students about their college search process. Near the end of our focus group, we passed around some marketing materials for them to react to — everything from brochures that had embossed logos or glossy logos, to booklets bound with real stitching and pieces with die-cut shapes. One piece I handed out had a cover made of clear plastic that looked like it was frosted in ice, and the center had been "scraped" clear to reveal a logo underneath. It was one of the most expensive and surprising printing executions we'd seen in years and we, the marketers, loved it. I was sure that high school students would think it was bitchin' (or amazeballs or whatever the current vernacular was for "really, really cool"). The first girl I handed it to stopped dead, got quiet, held it away from her body with both hands as if it might bite her and then said, with her face scrunched up like she was smelling something foul, "I feel like dolphins died for this." I almost blurted out a loud peal of laughter. *What?? Oh!* She thought the use of plastics and heavy inks wasn't environmentally conscious — that brands that used recycled paper were more her cup of tea. Duly noted.

Whether you're doing formal marketing or having a conversation with a new client, it behooves you to understand them as best you can. I'll say more on this topic in the following chapter, because it's important and bears further discussion.

WHEN RESEARCH IS PROMOTION AND DATA IS THE MESSAGE

Some companies hesitate to spend money on research because they want to conserve all their marketing dollars for "working media" (like the actual fees you pay to Google for a paid search campaign or the dollars you pay to a radio station for a series of commercials). But when done well, research IS promotion. Take, for example, mass surveys I've conducted that have left powerful impressions on the audiences about the sponsors. Sometimes thousands of people walk away thinking, "That was so cool how that company asked our opinions about their new products and wanted to understand us. I wish more companies cared so much about what the customer wants. I didn't really know about them before. I'm definitely going to check out their products." I also just conducted a small focus group on a college campus with parents who were craving a connection to the campus community. In 90 minutes, we had them feeling engaged and acknowledged in a way that no "we love and value you" email ever could have. The research was good marketing, even though that wasn't the primary objective. Think about how client/customer satisfaction surveys remind people how much they love you and then trigger them to refer new clients/customers to you. Research can be its own kind of marketing.

What some professionals never consider is that the data you unearth during your research can *become* the new story. When I worked in the graduate business school space, we wanted to be able to tell incoming students (all of whom were mid-career professionals already making good incomes) how their Lake Forest MBA would tangibly help them in their careers. I wanted to know how much more money our graduates were making; I wanted to tell a story in our marketing about the kind of success our alumni enjoyed. So, we asked. A major study with alumni across 50+ years revealed that "Within 3-5 years of graduating, the average Lake Forest MBA alumnus has achieved a 29% increase in total compensation." You can bet that research finding immediately found its way into our marketing messages (and into the hearts and minds of incoming and current students).

THE FUTURE OF MARKET RESEARCH

Most business leaders can't see the forest for the trees — or the roses for the leaves. You can find yourself working long hours to update your website interface to better serve the male customers you built your business to serve, not knowing all along that your product has incredible appeal to female consumers. But how would or could you know that? By asking. Market research is about asking the questions and asking them now.

Finish this sentence. "If only I knew ... about my customers, I'd be wildly successful." What is YOUR ellipsis? Ask and get the answers. I predict that more savvy business leaders will come to understand that a little market research can go a long way. I predict that leaders in every industry and in companies of every size will be asking "what's our ellipsis" — making wish lists and "things we think we know, but ought to confirm" lists. As for the really huge brands? Like mega-marketers at Target, other companies will fully leverage big data to understand what customers need and want, and will be able to know their customer behaviors better than those customers know themselves.

· ·

GETTING BACK TO THE PRINCIPLES

Market Research and the Think Like a Marketer Principles

Market research can be incorporated into your business in many ways and can impact your application of all five *Think Like a Marketer* principles. But it is the heart and soul of Principle #2.

Principle #2: Live and die by your customer insights

Market research studies come in every size and shape: big and small, simple and complex, frugal and pricy. The results? Game-changing. In nearly every single case. Trust that your market research projects will inform your day-to-day activities for years to come. Stop relying on marketing plans built on a wing and a prayer, and start developing strategies and plans built on real data. There's simply no reason to keep guessing when it's sometimes so easy to go get answers yourself. Making data-driven decisions drives bottom-line results.

. . . .

14

KNOW THY AUDIENCE

Living and dying by your customer insights (*Think Like a Marketer* Principle #2) means more than just conducting periodic formal research projects to get to know your customers. Really knowing them is about a relentless commitment to paying attention — to what the customers do and say (and what they *don't* do or say).

Be fascinated with your customers. Be enamored, smitten, curious. Never lose your interest in what they're thinking, what they need and what they care about.

Be fascinated with your customers. Be enamored, smitten, curious. Never lose your interest in what they're thinking, what they need and what they care about.

No matter how narrow your product or service offerings are, your customers are more complex and nuanced than you think. There is surely more than one "segment" of customers to be thinking about. By way of example, imagine you're a divorce attorney. It's easy to think you have one kind of customer — legally married adults in your state who are seeking a dissolution of marriage and don't know how to proceed and protect their own interests. But within that one large "segment" of clients are sub-segments — audiences with different needs, attitudes and means. There are clients with minor children and those without; clients with small business interests to protect; those with full- or part-time employment and those who are not working outside the home; there are female clients and male clients; straight clients and gay clients; clients who are angry and looking for a pit bull lawyer to help them "fight" and clients who are at peace with the separation, willing to let go of physical possessions and emotional grudges and just need your help moving forward into a promising future. The divorce attorney example can be extrapolated to any profession. Whatever kind of work you do, your customers probably don't comprise an audience that's as homogenous as your processes, culture and marketing practices might suggest.

Whatever kind of work you do, your customers probably don't comprise an audience that's as homogenous as your processes, culture and marketing practices might suggest.

In addition to having several audiences to serve, you must understand those audiences are constantly changing. Your primary audience, even if its demographic (like its average household income, residential geography or age) stays the same, will change behaviorally and attitudinally as time passes. I had the pleasure of conducting major market research with the "same" audience segment — college-bound high school juniors in major American cities — and doing that research twice (once in 2014 and again in 2018). Some of the shifts in general attitudes and expectations had changed in shocking ways. One example? In 2014, high school juniors wanted colleges and universities to treat them a lot like someone shopping for a new house or apartment — to focus on lifestyle, selling them on the housing amenities, the food options, the social activities on campus and the kind of people they'd be living with. Four years later, this very same demographic group was willing to sacrifice creature comforts to attend a higher education institution that delivered career results. They wanted high job placement rates, hands-on learning experiences and a reputation that opened doors. Audiences change ... even when audiences don't change.

AS YOU CHANGE, SO WILL THEY

Customers aren't the only ones changing. Your business is always in a constant state of evolution, too. As you change and grow as a company (and as you offer new products and services), you need to continually reassess who the right audiences are for you, what you know about them, what you *want* to know about them and how to best serve them.

LISTEN TO THEM, TOO!

If you've heard of a "listening strategy," but thought it sounded too fluffy to pursue, think again. Companies that have processes for listening, coupled with cultures in which they can activate on ideas they hear, are the companies that stay ahead of the curve. Renaissance marketers (those who are risk takers and smart strategists) literally re-engineer products based on what customers are telling them on social media and elsewhere. If you ever have occasion to bump into Jeffrey Hayzlett, global business celebrity and media host (and former chief marketing officer for Eastman Kodak), ask him about adding an external microphone to the Kodak Zi8 video camera based on customer suggestions (a simple idea that turned the

?? ASK YOURSELF ...

Have you done or said anything in the past year that could be construed as "tone deaf" by your primary audiences (e.g., customers, influencers, supporters, business partners)? Are you sure you're not doing anything right now to exclude or offend key audience segments that you could, instead, be delighting and serving?

product into that year's Christmas bestseller). First, you must listen and then you must react.

ONE CUSTOMER IS STILL AN AUDIENCE

Maybe you work with "audiences" of one customer or client at a time. Never lose sight of the fact that one customer is still a vital audience. Be constantly thinking about how to better know him or her, how to approach them, how to acclimate to his or her needs and how to guide them to a mutual goal. While your brand story might be stable and powerful, and your product offering firm, your delivery, tone and strategy for communicating might flex from customer to customer. Do you know how to customize your communications on a one-to-one basis? I was directing a photo shoot at a Chicago law firm when one of the attorneys, whose day was overscheduled and who was clearly not wanting to participate in the photos, resisted requests from fellow partners to step away from his desk to be photographed. I was told to give up trying — to leave him alone and accept the fact that firm photographs would be missing a key team member.

But I felt empathy for his resistance and didn't want to give up just yet. I shifted my approach to engaging him, offering him something special of value (some new headshots and lifestyle photos that would look like the cover of *GQ*), and his attitude shifted, too. His photos from that day are among my very favorites, and he and I have enjoyed a wonderful professional relationship since.

THE FUTURE OF AUDIENCE AWARENESS

The customer is your business. Without them, you are nothing. For the few companies who have yet to fully embrace this, the future is either very bleak or full of great opportunity. I predict that general business professionals — far beyond the walls of the marketing department — will learn to see every moment of communication (from presentations and speeches to media appearances and website copy) as an opportunity to connect with customers more deeply and to demonstrate their awareness of what the audience needs from them. As suggested in the previous chapter, big data and audience insights will continue to be big business (with big budgets). So, expect to see more and more senior management and executive positions with the word "customer" in the job title.

· ·

GETTING BACK TO THE PRINCIPLES

Audience Awareness and the Think Like a Marketer Principles

While "knowing thy audience" is the crux of *Think Like a Marketer* Principle #2 (Live and die by your customer insights), I'd like you to think about two additional principles.

Principle #1: Communicate for connection and meaning, not just to transact sales

Your business depends upon you truly understanding your customers. But if the only times you communicate with them are times you're focused on a financial transaction, you'll never discover all you need to know. Slow down, listen, connect. Understanding the practical concerns and aspirational dreams of the authors I work with helped me to know that they wanted to belong to exclusive, special "clubs" or affinity groups as writers. This understanding is what drove my decision to offer several publishing imprints: Silver Tree Publishing for non-fiction business books, Sterling Forest Press for literary books, and Silver Linings Media for memoirs.

Principle #5: Do everything in service of maintaining a virtuous cycle of creating value for the customer while capturing value for you

Creating value is about taking care of the customer. And to care for them, you must first know them and know them well.

. . . .

15

THE PRICE YOU PAY IF YOU OR YOUR EMPLOYEES ARE POOR COMMUNICATORS

Employees who can't communicate well can't open doors or close deals.

Everyone in your company — regardless of title and function and regardless of whether they are employees or contractors — are marketers. Your salespeople and customer service representatives are marketers. Your IT professionals, who maintain vital relationships with outside vendors, are marketers. CEOs, vice presidents and deans are marketers. Pastors, physicians and restaurant hostesses are marketers. And for this very reason, companies need to train themselves and their team members to be better communicators. Employees who can't communicate well can't open doors or close deals. If you're not investing in communications training — on becoming better presenters, better email and report writers, better company representatives on the phone and in person, and more persuasive professionals in general — you need to ask yourself why.

OPEN DOORS AND CLOSE DEALS

For much of my career, clients have been asking me to teach their people to "think like marketers" and to communicate more effectively. I'm frequently called upon by corporations to teach business writing seminars, communications boot camps and marketing workshops for employees who will ultimately use their communications skills (or lack thereof) when writing billboard headlines, reports for their board of directors, email memos to client prospects or language for their company website. I've worked with everyone from sales associates to scientists because effective communication is the basis for everything from sales success to FDA approvals.

But not all organizations — their CEOs or human resources departments or whoever makes the decisions about staff development opportunities — fully appreciate that training their people (up, down and across the organization) to be better verbal and written communicators is a high-impact way to reinvigorate their workforce with new skills that will impact the bottom line. In business, we are required to communicate. We lead meetings, distribute proposals, make phone calls, engage in hallway conversations, and send e-mails and instant messages. But are we doing it well?

Do you ever wonder ...

- If your communications are clear enough?
- Whether that e-mail you sent (when you were in a rush and not choosing your words carefully) might have inadvertently offended someone?
- How to deliver difficult news to an employee or customer?
- When to walk away from Microsoft Outlook and choose a face-to-face conversation instead?

- How to be more persuasive with your arguments so that your ideas will get the attention, results and funding they deserve?

If you care about your business and its results, you must first care about the communications skills of the leaders and employees who represent you.

Unless every single person in your organization is a practiced, professional communicator, you could probably benefit from regular training opportunities to teach things like brevity, clarity and persuasion. If you care about your business and its results, you must first care about the communications skills of the leaders and employees who represent you. Consider offering periodic seminars for communicators of all levels — particularly for those executives and professionals who don't think of themselves as "writers" or "public speakers" and for those in customer/client-facing roles like sales and leadership. Whether you're someone who writes documents and publications for external audiences, someone who writes a lot of internal reports and meeting minutes, or someone whose 8-hour day seems gobbled up by the composition of hundreds of little e-mail messages, even a handful of business writing or presentation tips could make a powerful difference for you. Being a better communicator is directly tied to your workplace effectiveness — to efficiency, job satisfaction, interpersonal relationships and revenue generation.

SWEAT THE DETAILS

At the risk of telling a story that might sound like a "tall tale," I need to tell you about how eager the average business professional is for modern-day grammar lessons. (*Say what?* I thought only wordsmiths and bookworms loved grammar!) When I started teaching corporate communications seminars, I always included some objectives and activities related to grammar (typically because someone in the client's HR department begged me to do so), but tried not to overdo it because I feared my participants would fall asleep. With that worry in mind, I developed what I call the "Grammar Game Show."

Picture this: A training or meeting room at your company, where a clothesline is tied the full width or length of the room, with laminated "cards" clipped all along the line. The cards are labeled with grammar and language topics, like "That vs. Which," "Who vs. That," "Rules About Commas," "How to Punctuate Bulleted Lists," "E.g. vs. I.e.," and so on. And rather than making otherwise confident and brilliant business professionals feel self-conscious about grammar "mistakes" they might be making or questions they should have asked 20 years ago, the teacher/student roles are reversed and the participants are calling the shots. I've got 60 minutes, a marker and a flipchart, and I've got to attempt to teach them 30 grammar lessons before we run out of time. (And yes, I almost always break a sweat!)

Engineers, CEOs and administrative assistants dash out of their seats, pluck a card or two from the line, hold it up and shout out their question, and we're off to the races. Thirty grammar lessons in 60 minutes or less. At every company I visit and for every industry represented, employees line up. When it's all over, they comment on the evaluation forms "More grammar please!" I was as shocked as you might be, at first. But then I realized that everyone has questions about language usage — things that trip them up at work and make them feel less confident; they've always wanted answers to their questions but never had the benefit of a safe, accepting venue in which to raise those questions in the first place. Offering communications training with some emphasis on the nitty-gritty gives employees what they've been looking for all along.

?!? ASK YOURSELF ...

Where are poor communications skills hurting you —
internally and externally? Have you done enough to improve
business outcomes by improving business communications?

THE FUTURE OF COMMUNICATIONS TRAINING

I predict that more organizations will come to realize that communications training is one of a few types of professional development
that can be offered in every department and for employees at every
level of responsibility to improve internal effectiveness (e.g., team
dynamics, employee satisfaction, project efficiency). Companies
will understand that everyone who communicates with customers,
clients or key vendors and partners needs to be clear, concise, kind
and persuasive when speaking, presenting and writing (even if
it's just a quick email or a hallway conversation).

I also predict that smart companies will invest in highly customized communications training (with industry or function-specific
programs, like persuasive writing courses for regulatory affairs staff
at pharmaceutical companies, or sessions tied to a company's brand,
like teaching staff to tell their story more effectively). More of these
learning opportunities will be offered virtually (like the series
of one-on-one communications coaching sessions I've developed for academic deans at the University of Wisconsin). And
training programs will become increasingly more vulnerable,
where employees — including those in the C-suite — aren't afraid

to address what they're afraid of (whether it's grammar, giving a presentation to the board of directors, or writing emails that deliver difficult news).

. . . .

GETTING BACK TO THE PRINCIPLES

Communications Skills and the Think Like a Marketer *Principles*

It could be argued that the ability to communicate effectively is tied to all 5 of the *Think Like a Marketer* principles, but let's focus on two that deserve your attention.

Principle #1: Communicate for connection and meaning, not just to transact sales

Develop a great story (see Chapter 2) and teach your entire team to tell it. First, your people must connect with customers, clients, partners and influencers; only then can you begin to sell. Strong communicators close more deals.

Principle #4: Create cultures and processes that align with your brand

The way you communicate, internally and externally, is the lynchpin of your institutional culture. Are you kind and clear, diplomatic and inclusive? Or are key communicators in your organization abrupt and accusatory, unclear and verbose, arrogant and secretive? Expect your professional communicators (e.g., your marketers, copywriters, media spokespeople) to have strengths in this area, but provide training to everyone. Know that the world will be taken by storm by technical experts who are stellar communicators — engineers and technologists who are eloquent and persuasive, and finance and salespeople who are "taking the numb out of numbers" (to borrow the title of a remarkable book by my colleague, Peter A. Margaritis). If you take steps to deliberately make your workplace one where clear communication is valued, supported and taught, you can't help but experience positive results.

. . . .

16

IF YOU ARE THE MARKETING DEPARTMENT, YOU'VE GOT TO THINK LIKE ONE

Vital Tips for Solopreneurs and Companies Without Marketing Leaders

If you're the founder of a small company or are a solo practitioner (like an accountant, attorney, physician or management consultant), thinking like a marketer may be more crucial for you than for the average business professional. If you're the proverbial "big cheese" (or the *only* cheese!), or if your company doesn't have a formal marketing leader and, therefore, the types of decisions explored in this book fall to you by default, it may help to take a moment to explore what "thinking like a marketer" looks like for lone leaders. It's up to you to make the mindset shift to think like a marketer to keep your business viable, relevant and strong. I hope these tips will help.

TIPS FOR WHAT TO INCLUDE IN EVERY YEAR'S PLANNING AND STRATEGY SESSIONS

Storytelling

(See Chapter 2.) Is your business story really your personal story? Think about what most impresses customers; maybe you're a physician and it's the fact that you did your residency at Mayo Clinic, or maybe you're an executive coach and it's the fact that all your clients are director-level and above at Fortune 500 companies. Find out what story your stakeholders like to share about you, and be sure you're giving them the information that will inspire their business and referrals. Don't forget to have a unique and well-articulated point of view on issues that matter to your customers. Resist cranking out a generic blog post every day to clutter social media feeds and email inboxes, but *do* have something strong, unique and share-worthy to say from time to time. If it's fresh and thought-provoking (and even surprising or startling), stakeholders will sit up and listen.

Sampling

(See Chapter 3.) If your business isn't as busy, efficient and/or profitable as you'd like (and let's not kid ourselves — why would you be reading this book if it was?), include time on your annual planning agenda to get serious about a sampling strategy. Remember, clients and customers can't know they love your product or service if they haven't tested it out.

Monetization

(See Chapter 4.) Be generous with your sampling, but know when and where to monetize. The only way you can keep creating value for customers is if you can afford to stay in business, so capturing value to the bottom line is imperative. Look at your prices and processes, and find fresh new ways to keep the cash flowing in. Consider offering your products or services in "tiers" (think of the Audi A4, A6 and A8). I am a strong believer in the motto: "Give them options, but not too many." There's a reason why some customers, who would get overwhelmed with the 57 toothbrush options at the grocery superstore and walk out emptyhanded, would then go to Sam's Club or Costco, where there are perhaps just two types of toothbrushes from which to choose, and then buy them in bulk. Too many options cause "decision paralysis" and too *few* options can make customers feel like they're being deprived of choice and control. Think about a "good/better/best" model for what you offer. Might that attract new customers and close more deals?

Lists/Databases

(See Chapter 5.) Customer relationship management (CRM) software is more nimble and affordable than ever, so don't let manual processes get in the way of collecting and using valuable customer data. Keep your lists up to date and clean; be unafraid to purge customers who are no longer contributing to the bottom line (or never were in the first place). And come up with realistic ways to manage this work if you don't have any support staff.

Try Some New Marketing Tactics

(See Chapter 6.) Try some new tactics if they fit your strategy — even if they're foreign to you and scare you a little. As a solo practitioner, it's easy to do things the way you've always done them. People at the top often don't take risks or try new ways of connecting with customers because there's no boss forcing them to do it. Force yourself.

Write a Book

(See Chapter 7.) For lone-wolf business leaders, writing a book can be a game-changer. It can elevate your brand, build celebrity, give would-be customers or clients great "samples" of your value, and open doors that were previously locked or too heavy. It's admittedly difficult to find the time for such a venture when you're a busy entrepreneur, but few business owners who take the book-authoring plunge end up regretting it.

Get Smart About Do-It-Yourself Marketing

(See Chapter 8.) Solo leaders make a lot of mistakes in this regard, feeling short on time and other resources, and getting lured into do-it-yourself or do-it-cheaply marketing activities that can actually cost you more — time *and* money — in the long run. Learn from the successes and mistakes of others in this regard. The ecosystem of products and services for marketing needs is constantly evolving. Try to keep up, but don't forget that if something seems too good to be true, it probably is.

Be Known, Be Seen, Be the Brand

(See Chapters 9 and 10.) Being "out there" — shaking hands, being known and being seen — is vital for one-man and one-woman shows (as is tooting your own horn). But be careful. The most obnoxious "look at me!" self-promoters are always the hungry entrepreneurs who don't realize that over-selling and over-promoting comes off as desperation, which eventually turns the customers away. Learn to connect with others in meaningful ways, believing in abundance for your business. My executive coach, Suzanne Coonan of Aerial Leadership, taught me many years ago that the worst thing I could do for my business is "operate from a mindset of scarcity" — taking every tiny bit of business, fearful that bigger opportunities weren't on the horizon. And she was right. While it's vital to "be known and be seen" and to help the marketplace understand the value you offer, desperation is never a good long-term business strategy.

Deliver Satisfaction Through the Right Kind of Delivery

(See Chapter 11.) Whether you sell services or products, there are inefficient ways and efficient ways to deliver them. There are ways that delight customers and ways that irritate them. Be thinking about what you distribute and how you handle those logistics now. Can you can sharpen your approach? Be thinking, as well, about "packaging" of products and even of your brand (e.g., there are some pretty awful websites out there for small companies and individual consulting practices). Make sure the *way* you deliver information, services and products is as classy, professional and awesome as you are.

Customer Service

(See Chapter 12.) Perhaps you have all the authority to make things right — to give a refund, to be generous, to take clients out to dinner, to go above and beyond. Then do all you can to apply the principles of this book to your delivery of stellar customer service. Be the very best in your sector, your market or your region.

Do the Research, Know the Customers and the Facts

(See Chapters 13 and 14.) Small business owners and solopreneurs are often the last people to do the market research they need to get the answers they seek. They're at the front line, so they're often blinded to what they don't know, either through arrogance or through the belief they don't have time to go find out. But there is always time. A simple customer/client satisfaction survey can give you the insights you need to make meaningful changes in your business that will show up quickly on the balance sheet. And really taking the time, as often as possible, to think about the different audiences you serve and what they need from you will make a significant difference in your business.

Sharpen Your Communications Tools

(See Chapter 15.) If you're a one-person company, you probably rarely, if ever, think about "employee training." Maybe the only professional development you gift to yourself is one great conference a year. But if that conference isn't focused on helping you communicate for improved business results, it might be time to think about how to be more deliberate about sharpening your writing, speaking, presentation and negotiation skills.

MARKET ONLY WHAT MATTERS

You cannot afford to market the wrong services or products. If you're a consultant to tech start-ups and you happen to be good at working with egomaniacal founders, but the act of doing so exhausts and depletes you, don't focus your marketing messages on nightmares and turn-around projects (or you'll keep attracting them). Market the wrong offerings and, suddenly, you'll be running a different business than what you intended. You'll be tied up running a business that evolved (or devolved!) because you made a decision about your website verbiage and case studies (or how you talk about your business at networking events) and because you did so without *thinking like a marketer.*

When you're a lone leader, it's also of paramount importance that you understand who the real decision-makers and influencers are (and I'm not just talking about the "consumer"). Very early in my consulting career, I was leading public relations and ghostwriting efforts for a renowned ophthalmologist who did "visual skills training" to teach professional and Olympic athletes how to improve their hand-eye coordination. After just a few months, my consulting contract was not renewed because, while the doctor himself was very pleased with my work, his office manager felt threatened by the degree to which the brand was being entrusted to me. She worked for the doctor, but he didn't know how to work *without her* and he was afraid of ruffling her feathers. So, while she wasn't technically my client, she ultimately called all the shots. I was out, and I didn't see it coming.

There are often other, unexpected influencers relevant to the decisions your customers make, and it behooves you to be aware of them. When a woman buys a car, she might be the *literal* customer but you'd be wrong if you thought that her in-laws, who visit only once per year but will need a place to sit when they're in town and getting shuttled here and there, might not influence her decision to go with the van or SUV that has a third row of seats. If you provide professional services, you might sell those services through the CEO's office, or the facilities department, or HR department, but depending upon how you describe yourself or how you handle the invoicing schedule, you might find that the influencers for whether you get the contract (or the fee you desire) are actually the chief financial officer or the head of purchasing.

THE FAST-FOOD APPROACH TO MARKETING: ANOTHER MINDSET SHIFT

In some ways, great marketing plans follow a fast-food model. Have you ever noticed how all the "new menu items" at Taco Bell are really just a remixing, repackaging and renaming of the same ingredients? Meat, lettuce, cheese, beans, salsa, sour cream and some sort of tortilla (corn, flour, soft, hard, flat, shell-shaped). Present it one way, and it's a burrito, another way and it's a taco, a third way and it's a salad. I suggest you think about your marketing assets like interchangeable ingredients. Think about what great assets you already have — what ingredients can be remixed and served up as new "dishes" to the marketplace.

Think about your marketing assets like interchangeable ingredients. Think about what great assets you already have — what ingredients can be remixed and served up as new "dishes" to the marketplace.

My client, Mimi Vold of Vold Inc., wrote up some incredible case studies and arguments about her brand during our brand storytelling initiative. How can she use those as the outline and basic scripts for marketing videos?

Rory Vaden, bestselling author of *Take the Stairs* and founder of Brand Builders Group has a brilliant method for creating a 6-minute, content-rich video that gets "remixed" and turned into blog posts, social media posts and more; it's the ultimate example of the fast-food approach to marketing (and it's delicious, by the way!).

Take a look at your best headlines and pull quotes on your website — that kind of pithy messaging often works perfectly on a highway billboard.

How might elements of a speech you delivered at a welcome event or open house or awards ceremony become the basic framework for a radio commercial?

Could the gorgeous photos you shot for street pole banners on your college campus also work as feature pages in a brochure to recruit new students?

How could the photos and headlines or key takeaways used in your LinkedIn Pulse articles be transformed into social media memes to build your brand, connect with customers or sell your products and services?

Even those of us who inherently understand the fast-food model of marketing can sometimes forget to use our best "ingredients." How many times have you sent your marketing team, a freelancer, your administrative assistant or yourself on an exhausting venture to create new content (for an article, a speech, a video, a radio commercial) when you already have incredible content that ought to be repurposed? In medium- and large-sized organizations, silos and poor internal communication drive this trend because no one is sharing. But if you're small, you know where all the assets are. If you want to produce a video for your website about your company's commitment to innovation, don't ask a copywriter to start from a blank page when drafting the script. Find your existing content — did the head of R&D recently give a great speech at a conference about the spirit of innovation? Is that a good place to start?

How many times has an agency crafted a brochure for you that's not even 20% as effective as your website copy? Right hands and left hands must know what the other is doing. Leaders who *think like marketers* will see marketing opportunities everywhere — they'll hear a customer say something on Twitter and think *we should interview them for a testimonial video,* or they'll be walking through the manufacturing plant and spot the perfect interaction between employees and know *this would be a great case study about culture and training for our HR team to use in our talent recruitment efforts.*

??? ASK YOURSELF ...

What makes you feel overwhelmed and out of your depths when it comes to marketing your company? Are you feeling more confident about how a mindset shift can enable you to generate better results? Do you feel more capable of leading the charge with marketing staff, contractors or agencies now? What growth can be spurred by thinking (and acting) like a marketer, and where do you still need help?

THE FUTURE OF THE LONE MARKETING MAVEN

If you own a small business or a one-person operation, marketing might be what you give the least attention to. If you had to write a job description for yourself, odds are that you'd forget to mention your responsibilities for marketing. But the pressure is intense and the responsibilities are real. Even when you're alone, you're not alone. Use this book to guide you, and be open to new ways of creating and capturing value.

If you had to write a job description for yourself, odds are that you'd forget to mention your responsibilities for marketing.

I predict that lone leaders will achieve future success by relying, more than they already do, upon on-demand agencies (for administrative support, for strategic and research services, for graphic design and for other creative services like writing). I predict such leaders will dedicate more focus to measuring their efforts and demonstrating return on investment, finally making the case (to others or to themselves) for hiring employees or contractors to own this vital work.

. . . .

GETTING BACK TO THE PRINCIPLES

Entrepreneurship and the Think Like a Marketer *Principles*

You're busy and you're pressed for time and money. You're just one woman or one man and, some days, you can barely keep up. When it all feels like too much, focus on these two principles:

Principle #3: Market in a way that's strategy-religious and tactic-agnostic

Focus on marketing activities that are arguably the most strategic, and stick with what's worked for you in the past, even if your buddy (who is also an entrepreneur) insists you need to be paying attention to a new-fangled, high-tech marketing tactic you know nothing about. Don't get distracted by shiny new objects. Be willing to try out some new tactics — if they fit your overarching strategy — but take the pressure off yourself. In an era when marketing departments have sub-specialists (like digital marketers and broadcast marketers and event marketers), it may be unrealistic to imagine you'll become an expert on every marketing tactic in the playbook. Just start by *thinking* like a marketer, and good things will follow.

Principle #5: Do everything in service of maintaining a virtuous cycle of creating value for the customer while capturing value for you

You've started a successful company and you know how to provide value to your customers. Never lose sight of doing that, but balance those efforts appropriately with decisions that allow you to capture more net revenue, more consistently. The more value you capture, the more likely you are to consider adding staffing or contract support to help you feel less alone in your marketing responsibilities. Good things are on the horizon for you.

. . . .

17

6 ENDURING TRUTHS ABOUT B2B MARKETING

(Which Also Happen to Apply to B2C Companies)

If your company sells its products or services primarily to other businesses (as mine does), this chapter about enduring truths in business-to-business (B2B) marketing was written for you. But, as luck would have it, these truths apply to business-to-consumer (B2C) companies as well, and I encourage you to think about applying a few, if not all, of them to your strategic planning and project planning for the coming year.

ENDURING TRUTHS

Enduring Truth #1

Your website better be your best sales tool. (And if it's not, quit driving people there!)

Why do so many brochures, banner ads, print ads, television and radio commercials, social media posts, and direct mail pieces have a call-to-action or hyperlink click-through to a crappy website? Business leaders of all stripes (including our beloved marketers), by default, think that the farewell section of a marketing tactic should include their web address and perhaps, though less and less these days, their phone number. But ask yourself, "If someone sees this ad and is intrigued, will a visit to our website be the experience that is *most likely* to turn them into a customer?"

Often, the answer is "no."

There's a lesson to be learned from the Tempur-Pedic mattress ads (on television and online) about "ask your friends." Those energetic, relatable ads didn't tell you to go to their website, because they know that word-of-mouth is their best sales tool. (Incidentally, see Enduring Truth #4. Tempur-Pedic understands this enduring truth, too.) Tempur-Pedic is a brand that puts the customer first in their marketing and doesn't rely exclusively on a website to sell a product that really requires recommendations and a "test drive" of sorts. Recently, I saw a new Tempur-Pedic commercial on television. The final call-to-action? "Visit a Tempur-Pedic retailer to learn more!" Indeed ... because often, the best salesman is, well, an actual salesman.

Often the best salesman is, well, an actual salesman.

But that's not to say you should ignore the importance of your website just because you're encouraging customers to engage elsewhere. Even if you're *not* driving people to your site, people will visit it because the internet is the default way to research products and services. At a Business Marketing Association conference a few years ago, I heard Jim Lecinski of Google say that 60% of B2B searches involve just one or two brands. That tells us that buyers already know who they think they want to talk to. They are ready to reach out and maybe even purchase from you. Your website will either reassure them that they are on the right track or turn them away forever. Try not to blow it.

Once your website is a thing of beauty, put those multi-media assets and messages to use all over the place. Lecinski urges marketers to "export" key elements of their website to where their target customer is. And when it comes to great websites, it better rock on mobile. Nearly half of B2B searches are conducted on mobile devices, so if you've been thinking "No one shops for roofing supplies or project management software from their mobile phone," and you've used that myth as an excuse not to optimize the mobile experience for your B2B customers, now you know better. B2B buyers are busy professionals, and busy professionals do research and business from their phones and tablets.

Incidentally, this fresh thinking about not always using your website as the default destination for B2B marketing applies equally to agencies and consultants as well, which is why I'm always looking to update our websites with fresh content and sharper messages about what we do and why it matters. As for whether the websites for my own business brands are my *best* sales tools? Absolutely not. My call-to-action with prospective clients is always "give us a call" and even "feel free to chat with one of our current or former clients, who can give you the inside scoop on our value." Because I know that nothing will convince someone to partner with me and my colleagues better than an in-depth conversation about their business challenges and the ideas we have about how to solve them (or in the case of the authors who choose our publishing company, very little compares to talking to an ecstatic book author who had a great experience with us). A website simply can't do that.

Enduring Truth #2

If you're not talking to Millennials, you're wasting your breath (and your money).

Approximately half of B2B decision makers are now only 18-34. They are the primary B2B audience, and yet most companies are still focusing their marketing strategies and messages on 50-year-olds. What in the world does this mean for the way we advertise and market? A great deal.

While younger Millennials often don't have the budget authority to make final decisions about whether to buy your products or services, they are the ones bringing the proposals forward and telling their leadership team, "We should buy XYZ project management software." Or "I think we should schedule a demo with Acme Engineering because they have the best-rated backhoes in the industry."

For kicks, I took a look at the age demographic of the customers visiting the Silver Tree Communications website and was startled to find that this trend applies to my primary business as well. (Go figure.) More than 1/3 of our website visitors are aged 34 or younger (though most of our new clients are *not* 34 or younger). It used to be easy for me to believe that the only customers who mattered to us for prospecting purposes were the 60-year-old CEOs and 50-something marketing directors and middle-aged authors with whom I work every day. But in thinking that, I would have been wrong. These people don't always find us on their own. Their directors, managers and executive assistants are visiting our website in droves and, no doubt, influencing the CEO, CMO, or director's decision.

As for how to customize your messages and online experience for Millennials? Be relevant, be modern, be accessible, be real.

Millennials were born in a digital age and have little tolerance for lead-capture forms that ask for too much information, or for slow-loading graphics or other suboptimal online experiences. What's more, Millennials who influence B2B purchasing decisions are savvy. They ask nuanced questions. They want to see how you stack up against your competitors, and they want to know what kind of support they'll get from your company once they make their purchase.

Be relevant, be modern, be accessible, be real.

Enduring Truth #3

Relevance is everything.

In many ways, this lesson is tightly linked to Enduring Truth #1 because relevance online is critical. But as the keeper of your company's brand, you should know that relevance *everywhere* matters.

I once sat in the audience when Russell Glass, founder of Bizo and subsequently head of products, LinkedIn Marketing Solutions, made one of the most compelling — and downright frightening — arguments I've ever heard at a marketing conference. In short, we have an *imperative* to be relevant to our prospective and current customers. With predictive analytics and other tools at our disposal, we should be embarrassed when our marketing completely misses the mark. We should know better. (Which reminds me that I've been getting beautiful, expensive membership recruitment kits from the direct response folks at AARP since I was about 33, never mind that my birth date is a matter of public record and I am not eligible to join their organization until I'm 50. AARP has an absolutely phenomenal, and surprisingly hip, social media program, so this isn't a brand that doesn't know how to market or reach its constituents. It's just another case of eye-catching marketing that is perfectly irrelevant to some of its recipients. I hope, for the sake of their budget, I'm one of only a handful of people for whom they are getting this wrong. I also hope they'll read Chapter 5 for some tips about lists and databases!)

Website visitors, by and large, tell companies, "You aren't relevant." How do we know? According to Glass, 90% of people who visit a website leave without converting (giving you their contact info in some way); 20% who convert will open your emails; and emails have a paltry 1% success rate in achieving their sales aims. That's a *lot* of waste. If your most recent marketing campaign drove 10,000 new visitors to your site (not bad, right?), that means just two (2!) people will end up buying your product or service. Let that sink in for a moment.

I recommend that you spend some time this quarter investigating predictive analytics, asking yourself, "What do we already know about our customers? What can we find out? (See the lessons about market research in Chapter 13.) And how can we create the right online experiences for them that are uber-relevant and drive conversions?"

Then ask yourself how your brand can be more relevant on mobile. A quick look at your website analytics will let you know what percentage of your visitors are accessing your site via a mobile device and, if your business is anything like most, this number will be 30% or even significantly higher. It can also be argued that the stakes are greater on mobile; if I send you an irrelevant ad on a website or in email and you see it on your PC, it's fairly easy to ignore or delete. But if I send you an irrelevant ad, notification, email, text or tweet to your mobile device and you pull your phone out of your pocket or purse in the middle of a board meeting to find out, I'm wasting your time. *Uh oh.* I've just been downright intrusive. If I do that too often, your perceptions of my brand are going to be incredibly negative. I'll go from being a brand you might want to interact with to one you consider a pest. Not good.

So, keep pushing for relevance. How can your company emulate what Amazon does — where they have created arguably the best online shopping experience because the experience (with its product recommendations based on my actual needs and behaviors) is unique to me and different for you? How might you reach for that star?

Personally, I love interacting with brands that care about relevance — I love shopping with Zulily because they don't waste my time showing me toddler clothing for the kids I don't have, and I've loved checking out new sleepwear from Adore Me because they never showed me a product (in my custom "Show Room") if it wasn't available in my size or preferred style. I recently heard someone say that their six-year-old complained when he saw an ad on his tablet for a video game, saying, "Don't they *know* we already own that game?" We're approaching a world in which everyone — aged 6 or 60 — will demand that kind of relevance.

Enduring Truth #4

Customers don't know whether to believe you.
But they trust their friends.

I think all marketers and business leaders instinctively know this. But there's a difference between understanding it and harnessing the power of this truth.

Even the best advertising always sounds like, well ... advertising. Our customers are wise to it. And they don't believe us. *Of course* we say that our products and services are the best ever!

Our university? World class!

Our IT consultants? Deep experts with outstanding customer service.

Our widgets? The most reliable and cost-effective widgets you've ever seen!

Even the best advertising always sounds like, well ... advertising. Our customers are wise to it. And they don't believe us.

This topic could be a chapter topic all its own, so I'll leave you with one important recommendation: read *Contagious: Why Things Catch On* by Jonah Berger. It will change the way you think about your business and the power of customers in driving business growth. Word-of-mouth doesn't just happen. Case in point: You think it was an *accident* that Coca-Cola decided to put "Share a Coke with Kate" on the side of a bottle to get people to start photographing and sharing (literally and virtually) sugar-water, far and wide? I'm a freaky "clean eater" and don't drink soda of any kind, but have bought three of those damned bottles — a Sandra for my mom, a Heather for my former assistant and a Magdalena for the adorable little girl next door.

Enduring Truth #5

Nothing inspires a customer like a great story.

Oh, how I love a great story. It's what I spend most of my time doing — creating and analyzing strategic and powerful brand stories — and it's why I opened this book with a chapter on strategic storytelling.

Every product or service — no matter how technical or seemingly mundane — should have a story. And the story should be memorable and *relevant* to the customer.

When I heard him speak to an audience full of marketers, Jonah Berger reminded us that business growth happens when people share your stories and that the concept of story is key. He joked that when people curl up at night with their kids, "Nobody tells bedtime facts ... " Good point.

Funny stories are memorable. Emotional stories are even better.

Enduring Truth #6

We live in an "experience economy."

Think about your life — about what matters most to you and about what you most enjoy spending your hard-earned cash on. If you're like most people, you care about the way you spend your time, and you treasure the memories you make with friends and family doing activities you enjoy. Stuff is stuff, but an experience becomes a memory forever. Whether it's snorkeling in the Virgin Islands or gambling with buddies in Las Vegas, great experiences almost never feel like a "purchase" decision. We can learn from that as business owners, leaders and marketers.

?!? ASK YOURSELF ...

Do you believe in the enduring truths outlined in this chapter? How well are you measuring up to these realities, and where can you commit to making improvements in the coming year?

James Gilmore, co-author of *The Experience Economy*, insists that if you can get customers spending time with you, you can also get them to spend money with you. (That's why Las Vegas puts so much effort into attracting business professionals to host conferences in their city. Once people have spent time there, by choice or by force, they are more apt to come back and spend some money.)

But how do you make a B2B experience for your customers? That takes some out-of-the-box thinking, but when it's done well, it can generate huge successes. Review Chapter 3 for B2B "sampling" experience ideas. I'll also reference Case Tomahawk's Customer Center — a giant sandbox, where prospective customers get to come play with the equipment on 500 acres in Wisconsin. Did I mention that the sales close rate for customers who visit the Center is 80%?

We live in an era when stay-at-home moms and IT guys alike are participating in Tough Mudders and where friends and families are paying to get locked in "escape rooms" with seemingly no way out. Everyone loves a memorable experience. Our marketing should seek to give those experiences, whenever and wherever we can.

GO FORTH AND DO BETTER, MARKETING-MINDED FRIENDS

The lessons are clear:

- Your best "sales closer" is not usually your website.
- Your customers may be younger than you think.
- You have an imperative to be savvy in your relevance.
- Customers trust their friends more than they trust you.
- Stories unlock purchase intent.
- And creating experiences for your customers is a great way to earn their loyalty and their sales.

These 6 enduring truths are bound to apply to your business, in ways big and small.

THE FUTURE OF B2B MARKETING

I've always thought it curious how much distinction we draw between B2B and B2C buyers because, really, there's no such thing as a "company" buying anything. Purchases are made by people. Yes, they might be people who represent large companies, but those humans are making purchase decisions based on the same considerations that individual consumers do: *Is this product or service worth what it costs? Can we generate ROI from it? Does the company selling this to us have credibility and proven quality? Do I have time for this decision right now, or can I put off the decision to buy this until a later date?*

I predict companies that sell their products to corporate buyers will become more clued into the human factors that go into those sales, and that the divides between B2B and B2C marketers will continue to dissolve.

I also predict that companies will spend hard on experiential marketing because new customers were raised with the expectation they can touch, feel, sample and experience. When it comes to digital presence, even solopreneurs are running out of time for having a lousy website. Even with the best outside sales force in the world, your brand story lives on your website and in your social media presences; do these assets live up?

GETTING BACK TO THE PRINCIPLES

These enduring truths hit upon all five of the *Think Like a Marketer* principles. If there's a principle that is becoming a priority for you as you get ready to begin applying the learning of this book to your company and your work, try selecting one or more of the enduring truths that align to your priority principles, and work them into your "to do" list for the coming months.

18

CONCLUSION: THINKING LIKE A MARKETER ... IN THE REAL WORLD

We've explored a great deal together in this book and, as the book and the journey both come to a close, I'd like to invite you to stay connected — to the 5 *Think Like a Marketer* Principles I know you are ready and eager to apply, to one another (through the *Think Like a Marketer* community on Facebook), and to me (see a great many ways to connect with me on page 245).

It's easy to get caught up in the firefighting and tactical pressures of business and forget to *think like a marketer.* I understand all too well. In truth, I wrote this book as much for *me* as I did for you — because even though I *am* a marketer, sometimes the need to move quickly causes me to misstep. I literally ask myself — several times a day (and yes, I ask it of my teammates, too) — *If I was really thinking like a marketer, would I make this decision? What might I do differently?* Thinking like a marketer is my business-decision governor; it keeps me from going too fast, veering too far or slamming on the brakes when I ought to keep going. I hope the philosophy will keep you speeding toward the right finish lines, too — toward delighted customers and profitable growth.

I encourage you to pin up a copy of the 5 *Think Like a Marketer* Principles near your desk or wherever you do their best thinking, to anchor you in the commitment to create and capture more value. (Visit SilverTreeCommunications.com/5Principles for a small poster to print and share.)

BE YOU, WITH A MARKETING MINDSET

When you decided to read this book — and perhaps it was at the urging of someone who recommended it — you may have been skeptical or even resistant. Perhaps you were thinking:

But I'm an accountant, Kate. I'm not a marketer.

But Kate ... I'm a physician — I am too busy seeing patients to think about how to market my practice.

But Kate ... I run a busy restaurant — you expect me to be a marketer, too?

No, I don't expect you to be a marketer. Not one bit. But you absolutely MUST open yourself up to the idea of thinking like one. And now you have.

You have opened yourself up to the idea of being the resident expert on customer insights. Opened yourself up to being the driving force behind your organization making big leaps — like changing your messaging to respond to the needs of the marketplace. Or like rethinking your pricing model. Or like evolving your organization's entire philosophy on sampling, distribution or tooting your own horn.

Remember that having a marketing mindset is not about becoming someone else or abandoning what makes you uniquely talented already. It's about adding a dimension that helps you make better decisions and relate more effectively to others.

Remember that having a marketing mindset is not about becoming someone else or abandoning what makes you uniquely talented already. It's about adding a dimension that helps you make better decisions and relate more effectively to others.

Marketing is science, and it's business. But it's only fair to admit that there's an element of art to the practice of marketing and a whole lot of gut instinct, too. Some days, I am able to make smart decisions even without the data to support those decisions, because I've been doing this for 20+ years. There are things I know *in my gut*, as they say. What's exciting for you and your organization is that after you've made the mindset shift to think like a marketer, your gut will become more reliable, too. Over time, after even a few months, and certainly a few years, of thinking like a marketer, you may find that you can count on your instincts more than you could in the past. You will know, even without the data or proof, what's likely to work for your customers or your marketplace or your product or your brand or your story (and what won't work) in a way that you didn't use to. Thinking like a marketer will have changed you for the better — made you a stronger leader, a more insightful innovator, and a more resilient force against changes in your industry, the economy and the social environment.

THE FUTURE OF THINKING LIKE A MARKETER

My last prediction in this book is one I surely hope will come true. I predict that thinking like a marketer — and the stories and recommendations shared in this book — will not just teach you some tips and tricks of the marketing trade, but that it will also connect you to:

- New ways of thinking about your business, your customers, and fresh ideas about how to create and capture value

- One another, as you seek out others who understand the power of thinking like a marketer

- Your company's culture, purpose, story and soul

- New opportunities to ignite profitable growth.

??? *ASK YOURSELF ...*

Remember those little viewfinder toys we had as children? You know, the ones you held up to your eyes and then pressed a plastic and metal lever on the right side — remember the sound it made, that satisfying mechanical "chit chit?" — to advance the wheel of photo negatives so you could reveal something interesting?

Barnyard animals or puppies or beautiful flowers or busy cityscapes. Those viewfinders were magical because they helped us SEE things anew. To perceive the world, even if momentarily and artificially, in a new way.

ASK yourself ...

What can you do — as a business owner or business leader — to see things anew? To catapult your company or ignite sales? To double your Net Promoter Score because customers love you so much they can't wait to tell their friends and colleagues about you? To *think like a marketer*, every day and every time it can serve you and your stakeholders?

Thinking like a marketer is ultimately about seeing the world of business differently. It is my hope that this book has given you new lenses with which to see the success and opportunity that awaits.

Welcome to a new vantage point.

THINK LIKE A MARKETER
5 PRINCIPLES TO GUIDE YOU

Thinking like a marketer requires that you:

1. Communicate for connection and meaning, not just to transact sales

2. Live and die by your customer insights

3. Market in a way that's strategy-religious and tactic-agnostic

4. Create cultures and processes that align with your brand

5. Do everything in service of maintaining a virtuous cycle of creating value for the customer while capturing value for you.

KEEP IN TOUCH!

🌏 **Learn more about the book, and quickly link to all the social media channels:**

ThinkLikeAMarketerTheBook.com

✉ **Send an email:**

Kate@SilverTreeCommunications.com

@ **Find, follow and share on social media:**

Facebook.com/Groups/ThinkLikeAMarketer
Twitter.com/KateColbert
LinkedIn.com/in/KateColbert

🎁 **Mail or ship something special to:**

Kate Colbert
6121 108th Avenue
Kenosha, WI 53142

📕 **To order books in bulk and learn about quantity discounts:**

Send an email! Interested in ordering 25 or more copies of *Think Like a Marketer* for your organization, association, conference or to distribute to clients who are business owners and leaders? Inquire at Kate@SilverTreeCommunications.com.

🚀 GO BEYOND THE BOOK ...

Hire Kate to:

- Create, build or protect your brands
- Conduct market research to find game-changing insights
- Guide you in developing the right story and the right strategy for sustained success
- Train you and your teams to be more effective communicators, at every level and in every circumstance
- Deliver a keynote or workshop experience on the *Think Like a Marketer* approach to leadership

Get the conversation started at 262-891-3290 or Kate@SilverTreeCommunications.com.

ACKNOWLEDGMENTS

It would be easy to imagine that, for a professional writer, writing a book would be a simple, natural adventure along a road that could be traveled relatively alone. And while there's a *tiny* bit of truth to that, the real story is a story of partnerships, saviors, cheerleaders and expert advisors. There are so many people without whom this book could not have been what it is, and without them, it could not have arrived so quickly in the hands of its readers. I owe a debt of gratitude to so many people. I will do my best to acknowledge many of them here.

First, **to my husband, Robert Colbert**, who made the largest, daily sacrifices during this process. There were moments many spouses could not have imagined or easily tolerated (like when I stayed on a cruise ship, working on the book, while he explored a Caribbean island without me), and his support was unflagging for months on end. *Honey*, for all the meals you cooked, all the early mornings you attended to the pups while I was sleeping off a "book author's late-night hangover," and for all the time we missed together while I worked 18-hour days, 7 days a week to make this book possible, I owe you — big time. And *I love you dearly.*

This book is stronger because of the efforts of **my outstanding editorial board — Karen Abruzzi, Cathy Fyock, Sara Skoog and Barb Wang**. Your honesty, fresh ideas, compliments and challenges brought me from "completed manuscript" to "ready to publish"

— from good to great. The generosity you extended by taking the time to read and review this book in its draft form is something I will never forget. *Thank you.*

The production and promotion of this book involved the very best publishing team ever. **To my extraordinarily talented art director, Courtney Hudson**, for designing incredible covers, typesetting the book to create such a classy and enjoyable reading experience, and designing incredible marketing materials for the book launch — *thank you* for making me and my work look so good, for being the yin to my yang, for being the very best creative partner imaginable. **To my expert and big-hearted editor, Hilary Jastram,** for enthusiastically jumping into this work — for your eagle-eyed attention and your joyful support every step of the way. *You are a gift.* **To my strategy-minded, budget-focused and eminently lovely book publicist, Stephanie Feger,** for believing this book could connect with audiences so quickly and completely, and for having the energy and courage to challenge me — a fellow marketer — about how to market my book. Every piece of sterling advice you have offered has made me, this book and this process better. *It's hard to imagine we ever got along around here without you; you are a treasure.* And **to my digital marketing maven and newest collaborator, Sarah Campos**, for building my awesome new website and preparing me for the book launch experience when time was tight, and I was full of visions that needed miraculous execution. *I have always thought you represent what is good and innovative and possible in the marketing profession; it has been a true treat to benefit from your talents.*

To my endorsers and early readers — those incredible men and women who lent their time, opinions and names to the Praise section of this book — you wow me and humble me. *I thank you, and I look forward to somehow returning the favor.*

I am largely indebted **to my book coach, Cathy Fyock**. She kept me motivated, accountable and on schedule. She never let me feel alone during the process, and she introduced me to an incredible community of fellow authors, with whom I was so honored to share this experience. It's not just that "books are magic," *Cathy — you are magic, too.*

To the members of my book launch team — too numerous to list here, but precious to me. You are the definition of goodness rising, of unflagging support, of generosity of spirit. Every social media post you made, every word of kindness you extended my way, every time you thought to recommend the book to a friend, colleague or stranger — I will wonder always if I deserved it, and I will remain in your debt for being my tribe when I needed you most. *I appreciate you deeply.*

To my photographer, Daniel LaBelle, and my beauty team, Jenny Kreye, Sheena Ashmore and Teresa Martinelli, for transforming me for the camera and capturing the real me — the seriousness, the silliness, the gratitude — so that my readers could know me better, *thank you.* In some ways, writing the book was the easy part. The vulnerability of the photo shoot required that I assemble the perfect team to make me comfortable and confident. *Daniel: You, in particular, have been such an important part of my professional journey these past several years; I am blessed to have shared so many pivotal moments with you.*

To my authors — the men and women who trusted me to publish and manage their books through our Silver Tree Publishing and Sterling Forest Press imprints — *thank you* for encouraging me to "sample" my own product by publishing my book just as you did. Thank you for your powerful and ultra-relevant advice and support along the way. You are the pros — I follow in your footsteps.

To all my clients who cheered me on and extended themselves graciously when I was so very busy. I am in awe of how many of you took the time to ask "How's the book coming along?" and "When can I buy a copy?" even when your highest priorities were your own pressing deadlines. I hope this book, which was inspired by your companies and your own collective character, does you proud. *You and your dynamic projects (and ambitious spirits) are what drives me every day.*

To my mom, Sandy Reynolds, who has tolerated an "absent daughter" while I was eyebrow-deep in this work, who asked me every single day how things were going (and who really, truly cared that they were going well!), who charitably served as the final proofreader of this book, and who gave me more "atta girls" during this process than any daughter could rightfully hope for, I am so thankful. *I love you. You are my everything.*

To my brother, Michael Whiston, for buying one of the very first copies of the book (which, admittedly, made it all feel so REAL!), and **to my entire family** — father, aunts, uncles and cousins who were kind enough to ask "So, what's your book about?" and then not act disappointed when they discovered it wasn't a riveting mystery novel. *Thank you!* There will be wine and delicious food at the book launch party, and I promise to talk about something other than the book during our holiday gatherings.

To all my friends, near and far, who have cheered me on, believed in me, and who are already reading and recommending the book to others, my life is better because you are in it. *Thank you for the smiles and for the love.*

To all the professors and writing partners who have taught me and inspired me over the years, I suspect you never thought all that time in literature courses and creative writing workshops might lead me to publish a business book (!). Every critique, every lesson, every moment of your time has led me to where I am today — a writer who builds brands and businesses, a storyteller whose stories generate revenue, an accidental marketer who couldn't be more thrilled with how her life turned out. *Thank you.*

And to all those companies and professionals whose stories I shared here — some by name and others anonymously — so that countless business leaders and owners could learn to "think like marketers," *thank you.* The work you do and the brands you represent have made my life a fascinating tapestry. Keep doing your amazing work — there is still so much value to create, so much value to capture.

ABOUT THE AUTHOR

Kate Colbert is an accomplished marketer, speaker and communications consultant who has led marketing initiatives for brands big and small, global and domestic. She is regarded as an eminent strategic storyteller with the ability to connect business and academic brands with enthusiastic and loyal customers to generate sustained, profitable growth.

Kate founded Silver Tree Communications, a full-service brand marketing consultancy, in 2002, and its sister company, Silver Tree Publishing, in 2015. She has expertise in leading the marketing efforts of brands in higher education, healthcare, professional services, consumer retail and other industries. She is best known for her groundbreaking work in market research and brand story development, her award-winning work in turning corporate data into actionable reports for high-stakes industries, her collaborative spirit in publishing impactful and inspiring books for new and established authors, and her leadership in working with employee groups (from scientists to technologists, C-suite executives to sales professionals) who seek to be more effective communicators. Kate is also a sought-after media spokesperson and crisis communications consultant, and a dynamic speaker who delivers presentations on communications and marketing topics.

Kate lives in Kenosha, WI, with her husband Robert and a pack of dogs she absolutely adores. When she's not working, she loves to travel, to volunteer for local charities and to read. *Think Like a Marketer* is her first non-fiction business book.

Made in the USA
Columbia, SC
26 August 2018